What Gods' Love Got To Do With It?

Remember what you do not understand you will misuse and abuse!

By
Pastor James L. Monteria

CLM Publications, LLC
P.O. Box 932 Chesterfield, VA 23832

WHAT GODS' LOVE GOT TO DO WITH IT?

REMEMBER WHAT YOU DO NOT UNDERSTAND YOU WILL MISUSE AND ABUSE!

All rights reserved. No part of this book may be reproduced without written permission from the publisher except for use of brief review for further of the Kingdom of God unless otherwise indicated, all Scriptures are taken from the King James Version of the Bible

CLM Publications, LLC

P.O. Box 932

Chesterfield, VA 23832

www.CLMPublications.info

ISBN: 978-0-9821450-3-6

Cover Design/Graphics: Shelly E. Middleton

Author: James L. Monteria

Associate Editor: Lisa Jones

Published by CLM Publications, LLC

Copyright © 2010 by CLM Publications, LLC Printed in the United States of America; All rights reserved under International Copyright Law. Contents and cover may not be reproduced in whole or in part in any form without the expressed written consent of the publisher.

Table of Contents

Devotional on the Commandment of Love

Introduction	Page	1
1. The Law of Jesus	Page	2
2. Commandment is not a Suggestion	Page	5
3. Understanding God's Love	Page	8
4. Do you know how much God loves you?	Page	11
5. It's so easy to Love Him	Page	14
6. The Purpose of the Change	Page	17
7. God's Love is poured out in our Hearts	Page	20
8. Love God with your Entire Being	Page	23
9. Learn to Love Yourself	Page	27
10. Love without Limits	Page	30
11. Encouragement - You can do it	Page	34
12. Operate with your New Heart	Page	37
13. You prove you Love God by loving Man	Page	40
14. We are Bankrupt without Love	Page	43
15. The Most Excellent Way	Page	46

Table of Contents

DEVOTIONAL ON THE CHARACTERISTICS OF LOVE

THE CHARACTERISTICS OF LOVE	PAGE	49
16. LOVE ENDURES LONG!	PAGE	52
17. LOVE IS PATIENT	PAGE	55
18. LOVE IS KIND!	PAGE	58
19. LOVE IS NOT ENVIOUS!	PAGE	61
20. LOVE IS NOT BOASTFUL OR VAINGLORIOUS!	PAGE	64
21. LOVE IS DOES NOT DISPLAY ITSELF HAUGHTILY	PAGE	67
22. LOVE IS NOT CONCEITED	PAGE	70
23. LOVE IS NOT RUDE	PAGE	73
24. LOVE DOES NOT ACT UNBECOMINGLY	PAGE	76
25. LOVE DOES NOT INSIST ON ITS OWN WAY	PAGE	79
26. LOVE IS NOT SELF-SEEKING!	PAGE	82
27. LOVE IS NOT TOUCHY, FRETFUL, RESENTFUL	PAGE	85
28. LOVE TAKES NO ACCOUNT OF EVIL DONE TO IT	PAGE	88
29. LOVE DOES NOT REJOICE AT INJUSTICE	PAGE	91
30. LOVE REJOICE WHEN TRUTH PREVAIL	PAGE	94
31. LOVE BEARS UP UNDER EVERYTHING!	PAGE	97
32. LOVE BELIEVE THE BEST OF EVERY PERSON	PAGE	100
33. LOVE IS FADELESS UNDER CIRCUMSTANCES	PAGE	103
34. LOVE ENDURES WITHOUT WEAKENING	PAGE	106
35. LOVE NEVER FAILS	PAGE	109

Table of Contents

DEVOTIONAL ON THE ACTIONS OF LOVE

THE ACTIONS OF LOVE	PAGE 112
36. LOVE YOUR ENEMIES!	PAGE 113
37. OVERCOME EVIL WITH GOOD	PAGE 116
38. PRAY FOR THOSE THAT GIVE YOU A HARD TIME	PAGE 119
39. STAY CONSISTENT WHILE UNDER ATTACK	PAGE 122
40. GIVE TO THOSE THAT WANT TO TAKE	PAGE 125
41. GIVE TO THE NEEDY	PAGE 128
42. PRACTICE BENEVOLENCE	PAGE 131
43. PRACTICE THE GOLDEN RULE	PAGE 134
44. LOVE THOSE WHO ARE HARD TO LOVE	PAGE 137
45. HELP THOSE WHO CANNOT RETURN THE FAVOUR	PAGE 140
46. GIVE FOR GIVING SAKE	PAGE 143
47. LIVING OUT YOUR GOD-CREATED IDENTITY	PAGE 146
48. SHOW MERCY	PAGE 149
49. DON'T PICK ON OTHERS	PAGE 152
50. DON'T CONDEMN THOSE WHO ARE DOWN	PAGE 155
51. BE EASY ON PEOPLE	PAGE 158
52. LIVE TO GIVE AND YOU WANT REGRET IT	PAGE 161
DECISION OF LOVE	PAGE 167
ABOUT THE AUTHOR	PAGE 170

Foreword

God's love! Only two words, but yet so infinitely powerful in their meaning. I believe the love of God is one of the most important messages in the Bible. The deeper I delve into God's Holy Word, the deeper is my understanding of what HIS love means for me as a believer. Everything that God does is a result of HIS love for us as HIS children. It is HIS unselfish love that gave us a Savior—JESUS CHRIST the Son of the living God Who shed HIS ever cleansing blood to redeem us. Still, do we as His children truly comprehend the love of God?

As the bible tells us that His ways are higher than our ways, and His thoughts are higher than our thoughts **(Isaiah 55:9)**, it is not surprising that God's love encompasses so much more than just His love <u>for</u> <u>us</u>. As Christians, He commands us to have His type of love for one another and the unsaved (commandment);

He expects His love to be exemplified in the way we conduct ourselves (character); and He expects us to consistently demonstrate His love towards others (action).

Yes, God has high expectations on His children regarding His love, but He has made provision for us. When a person accepts Jesus as their own personal Lord and Savior, the love of God is shed abroad in their heart giving them the ability to love as He loves.

This love gives purpose to life and a sense of self worth. It does not devalue people; it creates an appreciation for yourself and others. With the leading and teaching of the Holy Spirit, God's love will change the characteristics of our life. As we walk in love, the characteristics of God will be manifested in every area of our lives. We can become more connected to the things of God, no longer in bondage, doubting our purpose, being envious, hating and showing bitterness to our brothers and sisters. Oh, the power of His love!

His Word also reveals that the key to receiving and enjoying the blessings of God is tied to our walking in the love of God. We serve such an awesome God! His design is that as we obey and seek to bless and honor Him by carrying out His commandments.

we are abundantly blessed in return! Of course, this should not be our primary motivating factor for walking in God's love, but it is definitely a benefit to appreciate.

God is so in love with His children. Let's learn to show Him our love in return by obeying His commandment to love as He loves, producing Godly character in us and enabling us to demonstrate the most powerful force on earth to others - the love of God.

With the help of the Holy Spirit, I have created this booklet to give you a glimpse of the power of His love and to help you understand:

Remember

What you do not understand you will misuse and abuse!

- The commandment from God Himself to love as He loves

- How to develop your character by walking in His love

- How to be a living example of His love through your treatment of others

Are you ready to go higher? God is ready. Let us not keep Him waiting!

The one thing that causes more people to miss heaven than anything else is not having love for one another.

Devotional on the Commandment of Love
Introduction

I heard a Pastor tell the story of a man who had a vision from the Lord. In the vision, the man was attempting to hang big and beautiful curtains but the curtain rod kept falling down. He realized that the curtains had words on them and each word meant something. The curtains represented faithfulness, peace, favor, grace, etc. The man in the vision was frustrated because he could not get the curtains to remain in place. As he would work on one, another would fall. The man finally cried out to the Lord in desperation. The response the man heard was, **"Hang the rod!"** He looked over and saw a huge golden rod. The rod was big enough to hold all the curtains in place. The rod also had words on it that read, "The Love of God."

I may not have told the story exactly the way that Pastor Bill Winston told it, but the essence is there: in the Kingdom of God, everything hangs on the love of God. If you get the rod of love in place, then the curtains of faithfulness, peace, favor, etc. will hang in place as well. To try to receive the blessings of God without the love of God, however, can be a frustrating experience. Too many people are trying to get things from God without really knowing God at all. Don't pursue things, pursue God. If you pursue God and walk in love, the things (blessings) will come to you. Nothing else really works – at least not for long, without the love of God operating in your life. Jesus simplified the message of the Bible for us in two commandments: love God and love man. If you can do these two, then you are giving God His proper place, and you are, in effect, hanging the rod of love. Once you get love in place, everything else will stay in place.

1. The Law of Jesus
Matthew 22:37-39

"Jesus said to him, 'You shall love the Lord your God with all your heart, with all your soul, and with your entire mind.' This is the first and great commandment. And the second is like it: 'You shall love your neighbor as yourself."

I believe this quite possibly could be the most important passage about love in the Bible. In this passage, the Pharisees and the Sadducees made constant attempts to stump Jesus. They wanted to, somehow, trap Him into violating the Law. Here is a little back ground to help you understand. The first five books of the Bible are known to Jews as the "Torah" or, the "Law of Moses." The Law contained many commandments and it was literally impossible to live by them all. So, the Sadducees attempted to entangle Jesus in a legal dilemma by asking Him if it was lawful to pay taxes. Jesus knew it was a trap and He asked whose face was on the money. When they agreed that it was Caesar's face, and then Jesus said, "Then give Caesar what is his, and give God what is his." With this, Jesus silenced the Sadducees.

Since the Sadducees were unsuccessful at getting Jesus entangled in the Roman law, the Pharisees then attempted to get Him entangled in the Jewish law.

They brought forth their best lawyer (an expert in Jewish law) to ask Jesus this seemingly simple question: what is the greatest commandment in the Law? Jesus' answer had wide-spread application.

He first quoted Deuteronomy 6:5 which states, "And thou shalt love the Lord thy God with all thine heart, and with all thy soul, and with all thy might" elevating this to the greatest commandment. The Pharisees had only asked Jesus to identify the "one" top commandment, but Jesus went on to add a second one.

Jesus said that the second one was like the first one and it was to "**Love your neighbor as yourself**." This second commandment was not a quote from the Law at all. Loving your neighbor might have been a principle, but it became a law that day. Jesus went on to say that all the Law and the Prophets stand on these two commandments.

Summary

You don't have to remember hundreds of commandments or be a scholar in the Levitical law to live a life that is pleasing to God. Jesus made it easy for us by capturing the essence of Christianity in two laws: Love God and Love Man. We will see that they are both important, and if fulfilled, we will live a prosperous and peaceful Christian life. If you want to know the secret of how to live a life that is pleasing to God, then here it is: love God and love your neighbor. Fulfill these, and the rest will fall in place.

*** Notes: Lesson #1 Weekly Reading ***

2. Commandment is not a Suggestion!
John 13:34, 35

"A new commandment I give you: Love one another. As I have loved you, so you must love one another. By this all men will know that you are my disciples, if you love one another." I would venture to say that learning to walk in love is <u>one of the most</u> important facets of any Christian's life. I pray that this little book will be a blessing to you.

In John 12, Jesus made His triumphant entry into Jerusalem, marking the beginning of the end of His life. The feast of the PASSOVER was just a few days away and He would be the PASSOVER lamb, once and for all.

Jesus predicts His death in the latter part of the 12 chapter and begins to give His disciples the last teachings, prior to His crucifixion in chapter 20. In chapter 13, Jesus teaches His disciples a great lesson about humility by washing their feet. Later on in the chapter He says something very interesting.

For now, I want to focus on the fact that Jesus called loving one another a **commandment**. We will also discuss the types of love and why this commandment introduced a love that was new and completely different from any they had ever operated in before. A commandment is an order, direction, or requirement based on the authority of the person giving the commandment.

A suggestion is different. A suggestion is an attempt to influence without the qualification of authority. Jesus was not suggesting here; He was not attempting to simply influence them.

Jesus began His final instructions to His disciples by letting them know He required them to operate in the love of God.

This was not something that would be limited to the original disciples. We must see that no believer is exempt from this commandment. Most people understand commandments like "thou shalt not kill," or "thou shalt not steal;" but "love one another" is of equal, if not greater, importance! Remember that He does not merely possess love or operate in love. God literally is love according to 1 John 4:8. The word "Christian" means "like Christ." If we are going to be "like" Him, then we must operate in love.

Summary

Being a true Christian leaves you without an option when it comes to loving people. God did not qualify whom you should love by saying that you could love those you like and hate those you dislike. Neither was God suggesting that operating in love is a good thing to do if you get around to it. No! Love is a commandment; a requirement; an obligation, and, love is a lifestyle! Enter each day with a determination to operate in the love of God.

*** Notes: Lesson #2 Weekly Reading ***

3. Understanding God's Love!
John 13:34, 35

If we are to live out the love that Jesus spoke of, then we should make every attempt to understand it. You will always abuse and misuse what you do not understand. One of the first things we need to understand is that in English, we only have one word for love, but there are several words for love in Greek. Four of the Greek words for love are:

Storge: A family type of love. This is how you love your brothers and sisters.

Eros: A physical type of love. This is one way of showing your appreciation for your spouse by sharing a part of yourself. The world has become perverted and this type of love has become "erotic."

Phileo: This is a brotherly or friendly type of love. This word is the root word for Philadelphia and why the city is called "The city of brotherly love."

Agape: This is the word that was used when Jesus said, "By this all men will know that you are my disciples, if you love one another." This type of Love is based on a decision to obey the Word of God.

This is the type of love that we are focusing on; this is the type of love that we need to truly understand.

God's love requires obedience to His Word: "The proof that we love God comes when we keep his commandments…" **(1 John 5:3)**

A) **God's love requires love towards one another:** "…believe on the name of his Son Jesus Christ, and love one another…" **(1 John 3:23)**

B) **God's love requires love back towards God:** "The real test on whether or not we love God's children is this: Do we love God? Do we keep his commands?" (1 John 5:3)

Summary

Once you know better, God expects you to do better. God wants you to learn about His love and He wants your learning to turn into a way of living. He does not want you to say you love Him, but then fail to love others; or claim to love Him, but then fail to obey His Word.

God wants you to express your love for Him by allowing His love to flow freely through you this day and every day. Are you ready to face this day in the love of God?

*** *Notes: Lesson #3 Weekly Reading* ***

4. Do You Know How Much God Love You? Romans 7:14-25?

"For what I am doing, I do not understand. For what I will to do, that I do not practice; but what I hate, that I do." (Romans 7:15)

Paul admitted to dealing with the inner struggle we all face from time to time; the conflict between wanting to do right and the actual act of doing it. He then went on to give us hope in the opening verses of the 8th chapter by letting us know that our life in the Spirit can overcome the desires of the flesh.

Paul declares, "Do you think anyone is going to be able to drive a wedge between us and Christ's love for us? There is no way! Not trouble, not hard times, not hatred, not hunger, not homelessness, not bullying threats, not backstabbing, not even the worst sins listed in Scripture:

They kill us in cold blood because they hate you. We're sitting ducks; they pick us off one by one. None of this fazes us because Jesus loves us.

I'm absolutely convinced that nothing – nothing living or dead, angelic or demonic, today or tomorrow, high or low, thinkable or unthinkable – absolutely nothing can get between us and God's love because of the way that Jesus our Master has embraced us." (Romans 8:35-39).

As you desire to grow in the love of God, read these verses a couple of times per day and allow the Holy Spirit to solidify in your heart the height and depth of His love for you.

Absolutely nothing can stop God from loving you. You did nothing to make Him start and you can do nothing to make Him stop. Now, this is not a license to sin. He loves you just the way you are, but He loves you too much to leave you there. Remember that this passage of inseparable love is found in a chapter where Paul is teaching on living a Spirit-led life.

Summary

God loves you. Your assurance of God's love for you breeds a confidence that money can't buy and that the devil can't steal. God loves you with an inseparable and inexhaustible love. The God of the Universe takes the time to love you personally and intimately. Once you settle this in your heart, you will be able to face every day with a quiet conviction that enables you to overcome any obstacle.

*** Notes: Lesson #4 Weekly Reading ***

5. It's So Easy to Love Him!
Psalm 19:1 NIV

"The heavens declare the glory of God; the skies proclaim the work of His hands." David said that the heavens declare the glory of the Lord."

The clouds are a testament of His handiwork; the mountains an example of His strength, the sun an example of His power, and the moon an example of His wisdom. All of creation declares His glory. God was thoughtful enough to clothe a flower with beauty, to fill a pear with sweet nectar, to put healing virtue in herbs, to cause plants to exchange carbon monoxide for oxygen, and the list goes on and on. Who would not love a God like that?

According to Psalm 19:4 says "Their line is gone out through all the earth and their words to the end of the world. In them hath he set a tabernacle for the sun, put singing in a bird, and colors in a rainbow; He can surely meet your needs." Also, Peter told us to cast all our cares upon Him (1 Peter 5:7).

Why? Because He cares for us! Think about that for a moment. The God that watches over the universe cares about you, your family your children, your career, your desires, your plans, and your concerns. You may not have awakened with God on your mind, but I guarantee you that you were on His. He is mindful of you (Psalm 8:4) and He is never too busy to meet you where you are.)

Summary

After learning about the love of God, you may consider walking in love to be a hard thing. You may think that fulfilling all the requirements of God's love is unattainable, but I want you to know that loving God is not a difficult task. God is easy to love. He takes the time for you; you should simply make the time for Him.

Acknowledge Him today; His glory, His splendor, His power and His might. Know that the God that made everything takes the time to hear from you.

In Psalm 19:14, David prayed a prayer that applies to our lives today, "May the words of my mouth and the meditation of my heart be pleasing in your sight, O Lord, my Rock and my Redeemer."

*** Notes: Lesson #5 Weekly Reading ***

6. The Purpose of the change!
1 timothy 1:5 AMP

"Whereas the object and purpose of our instruction and charge is love, which springs from a pure heart and a good (clear) conscience and sincere (unfeigned) faith"

Paul had a great relationship with his son in the faith, Timothy. Timothy was his protégé. Paul's first letter to Timothy was a charge to continue the ministry that he started in Ephesus and to teach the right things. The people of that time period were focusing on legends, myths, and issues of race and ancestry.

Paul told Timothy that these discussions would only lead to arguments and would be unproductive in the Kingdom of God. Providing an excellent illustration for our text, Paul clearly charges Timothy to both operate in love and teach the people to love.

According to 1 John 4:8 states "He that loveth not knoweth not God; for God is love." This is the charge of Christianity, because God is love. We have been destined to be transformed into the image and likeness of Christ (Romans 8:29) and Christ's image is an image of love. With this in mind, let's take a look at the three areas of the charge to love found in our text:

1.   **A Pure Heart**: This charge is not a charge to simply have outward expressions of kindness, but to ensure that your actions are motivated by the love that you have rooted and seated in your heart. What is the motivation behind what you do?

Do you perform good works because you love or because you want to say that you did good works? God does not look at your outward actions; He looks at the heart (1 Samuel 16:7).

2. A Clear Conscience: It is hard to walk in clear and pure love with God and man when you are walking in guilt. Sin hinders our prayer life and clouds our conscience. T o truly walk in love you must be in right standing with God. If you are in sin, take a few moments to repent. John said, "If we confess our sins, he is faithful and just to forgive us our sins, and to cleanse us from all unrighteousness" (1 John 1:9). Make sure you have a clear conscience before you leave from whatever you may be doing.

3. Sincere Faith: When you make an attempt to walk in love, you are literally walking by faith. You are expressing your sincere confidence in God and in His Word. When people commit wrongful acts against you and you decide not to respond the way you used to because of what you have learned about God and His Word, you are expressing your confidence in the Word you received and you are walking in sincere faith.

Summary

Your name does not have to be Timothy to receive God's charge to walk in His love! God expects you to turn the corner from learning to living. You have been learning about God's love; are you ready to walk in love with a pure heart, a clear conscience and sincere faith? The choice is yours! If you choose yes, then you will also experience God's favor upon your life.

*** Notes: Lesson #6 Weekly Reading ***

7. God's Love is poured in Our Hearts!
Romans 5:5-8;

"…And hope maketh not ashamed; because the love of God is shed abroad in our hearts by the Holy Ghost which is given unto us. For when we were yet without strength, in due time Christ died for the ungodly. For scarcely for a righteous man will one die: yet peradventure for a good man some would even dare to die. But God commendeth his love toward us, in that, while we were yet sinners, Christ died for us."

Paul talks extensively about the faith of Abraham in the fourth chapter of his letter to the church at Rome and explains how his faith was "credited to him" as righteousness. In verses 23 and 24, Paul says "The words 'it was credited to him' were written not for him alone, but also for us, to whom God will credit righteousness for us who believe in him who raised Jesus our Lord from the dead." We can see that our righteousness is tied to Jesus the Christ.

Paul says that God "poured out his love into our hearts by the Holy Spirit." We receive the Holy Spirit when we receive salvation and a lot has been said about what we receive when we receive the Holy Spirit. Many focus on the power, authority, deliverance, and security, etc. That we receive; but one often overlooks a very important aspect of our salvation: we receive the love of God in our hearts when God Himself comes to live in us!

Our Heavenly Father demonstrated His love for us by sending His only begotten Son; Jesus demonstrated His love by dying on the cross for us while we were still sinners; and the Holy Spirit continually demonstrates His love by living in us and permeating the love of God in us and through our hearts.

Summary

Remember that the Holy Spirit lives inside of you as a born again believer. When the Holy Spirit took up residence in you, you received God's love (1 John 4:8). God is inside of you, and He has poured out His love in your heart. That having been said, shouldn't you want to walk in the love of God?

Knowing how God overlooked your faults and still loved you enough to save you should be motivation enough for you to look beyond some of the faults of others and still love them. You may not wear clergy attire, ever stand behind a pulpit, or ever stand before thousands; but you can love. The greatest example of godliness is when we love as God loved.

*** Notes: Lesson #7 Weekly Reading ***

8. Love God with You Entire Being!
1st Thessalonians 5:23;

"And the very God of peace sanctify you wholly; and I pray God your whole spirit and soul and body be preserved blameless unto the coming of our Lord Jesus Christ."

Take a closer look at the passage dealing with the first part of Jesus' instructions, "Love the Lord your God with all your heart and with all your soul and with your entire mind." Let's start with "Love the Lord your God…" The name used for God here is Jehovah. Jehovah comes from the past, present, and future tenses of the verb "to be;" meaning simply but profoundly, "I am who I am," and "I will be who I will be". In Exodus 3:14 it states "And God said unto Moses, I AM THAT I AM: and he said, Thus shalt thou say unto the children of Israel, I AM hath sent me unto you."

Jesus clearly lays out a requirement for all believers to love God; the God of our past, present, and future; The God Who was, and is, and ever shall be.

"**…with all your heart…**" Here is the three-fold nature of man: man is a spirit, has a soul, and lives in a physical body. The spirit is the dimension of man which deals with the spiritual realm, the part of man that knows God. The soul is the dimension of man which deals with the mental realm; his intellect, sensibilities and will combined producing thought and reason.

The body is the dimension of man which deals with the physical realm, the house in which we live.

The words "heart" and "spirit" are used interchangeably in scriptures. Your heart is your spirit. When the Word of God speaks about the heart of man, it is speaking of the spirit of man. Notice that 1 Thessalonians 5:23 doesn't just say "I pray God your whole heart….", it says, "…I pray God your whole spirit and soul and body….." When a person makes a decision to receive Jesus as their Lord and Saviour, their heart is changed and they love with all their heart or spirit. They must continue to love God with all their heart or spirit by daily spending time in prayer and reading their Bible. This is the way that you love God with all your heart or spirit.

"…with all your soul…" This is where you have your mind, will, and emotions. 1 Thessalonians 5:23 states "And the very God of peace sanctify you wholly; and I pray God your whole spirit and soul and body be preserved blameless unto the coming of our Lord Jesus Christ."

I believe that this refers to your will. God has given you the ability to choose. You are a free moral agent. You can choose to love or hate, bless or curse, worship or disregard.

You have the ability to choose, but when you submit yourself to God and allow Him through complete teachings of the Word of God – to transform you into His image and His likeness, then you simply choose what He would have you to choose. This is how you love God with your will. **"…with your entire mind."** In many ways, you are what you think you are.

This is illustrated in Proverbs 23:7 which states "For as he thinketh in his heart, so is he: Eat and drink, saith he to thee; but his heart is not with thee".

You are the way you think you are. If you think you can or you think you can't, you're right either way. If you can change the way you think, you can change the way you are. To love God with your mind is to train and transform;

In Romans 12:1, 2 says "I beseech you therefore, brethren, by the mercies of God, that ye present your bodies a living sacrifice, holy, acceptable unto God, which is your reasonable service. And be not conformed to this world: but be ye transformed by the renewing of your mind, that ye may prove what is that good, and acceptable, and perfect, will of God."

Your mind can be changed to think the way God thinks. You train yourself to think good thoughts and not evil. Your thoughts will lead to your actions.

Summary

The greatest commandment in the Bible is to love God with all your being. Love God with your heart (your feeler), your soul (your chooser) and your mind (your thinker). Once you start loving God this way, then you are on the road to becoming the person God intends for you to be.

*** Notes: Lesson #8 Weekly Reading ***

9. Learn to love yourself!
Matthew 22:37-39;

"Jesus said unto him, Thou shalt love the Lord thy God with all thy heart, and with all thy soul, and with all thy mind. This is the first and great commandment. And the second is like unto it, Thou shalt love thy neighbor as thyself."

There are many people, Christians included, who do not love themselves. I do not mean that we should love ourselves to the point where we have an unhealthy and unrealistic image of our character and abilities; but I do mean that we should be thankful to God for making us the way that He did. No one else on the planet has your fingerprint. No one else has your voice signature.

Your eyes are one-of-a-kind. This uniqueness is an example of the creativity and the intricate detail of God. He formed you like no one else. David said, "Oh yes, you shaped me first inside, then out; you formed me in my mother's womb. I thank you, High God – you're breathtaking! Body and soul, I am marvelously made! I worship in adoration – what a creation!" (Psalm 139:13, 14) - David praised God for making him the way that He did and so should we.

Let's get beyond some of the common hindrances:

1.) **Weight**: Lots of people consider themselves over weight and they do not like what they see when they look in the mirror. There is a healthy dissatisfaction that drives us to exercise, but then there is an unhealthy dissatisfaction that leads to low self esteem.

If this is you, then ask God to help you take control of your emotions. Develop healthy eating habits, exercise, and address your weight concerns; but most importantly, learn to love yourself. God loves you just the way you are and so should you.

2.) Past Failures: We all have made and will make mistakes. However, some people cannot seem to get beyond their past mistakes and failures. Most multi millionaires have filed for bankruptcy at least once. What does that mean? They learned to get past failures and to try again.

3.) Past Sin: This is a big one. Many Christians have come to God, repented, and received forgiveness. They know that God has forgiven them, but they have not learned to forgive themselves. Learning to forgive myself is a gift I have learned and a key to walking in peace.

Summary

You must learn to love yourself. God loves you just the way you are. This is not a license for sin, but it is a commandment to love. Learn to be thankful for the way you look, speak, laugh, and smile. Learn to love being YOU! No one else can be a better you than you. Get past failures yesterday ended last night; today is a new day, and you have new mercy.

Accept forgiveness from God and learn to forgive yourself. Don't beat yourself up about yesterday. Face today with great expectations! As you love yourself you will be able to love your neighbor!

*** Notes: Lesson #9 Weekly Reading ***

10. Love Without Limits!
John 21:15-17;

"So when they had dined, Jesus saith to Simon Peter, Simon, son of Jonas, lovest thou me more than these? He saith unto him, Yea, Lord; thou knowest that I love thee. He saith unto him, Feed my lambs. He saith to him again the second time, Simon, son of Jonas, lovest thou me? He saith unto him, Yea, Lord; thou knowest that I love thee. He saith unto him, Feed my sheep. He saith unto him the third time, Simon, son of Jonas, lovest thou me? Peter was grieved because he said unto him the third time, Lovest thou me? And he said unto him, Lord, thou knowest all things; thou knowest that I love thee. Jesus saith unto him, Feed my sheep."

The Greek word for God's love is **agape**. Agape love is superior to the other three types of love. We also discussed the fact that agape comes from God's Spirit. In other words, you cannot love God's way without God's Spirit. We will see how this applies to our lives. If you read the reference closely you see that Jesus asked Peter three times if he loved him.

Now that you know there are different words for love in Greek, you might be interested in knowing that the same word for love is not used in all three questions. The first two times Jesus asked Peter if he loved Him with God's love (agape).

Peter's response was, "Lord you know that I love you with brotherly love **(Phileo)**." The third question, however, was different. Jesus asked Peter if he loved Him with brotherly love **(Phileo)**.

This is where our text says that Peter was **"hurt"** by the question. Peter replied, "…you know that I love you." The word Peter used was Phileo (brotherly love), not agape (God's love). Why was Peter hurt the third time? I believe it was because he then realized his limitations. He had walked with Jesus for three years. He saw Jesus heal the sick, raise the dead, Jesus cause the blind to see, lame to walk, and deaf to hear.

Jesus never performed one miracle, however, until the Holy Spirit came upon Him at his baptism. Jesus did everything that He did for the Kingdom after the Holy Spirit – what Adam had in the garden was restored to Him.

Peter could not love Jesus with God's love **(agape)**, because he was not yet born-again of God's Spirit. God's love **(agape)** is a fruit of the Holy Spirit. "But the fruit of the Spirit is love, joy, peace, longsuffering, gentleness, goodness, faith," according to Galatians 5:22). So, in essence, when Jesus asked Peter the third time, "Do you love me **(Phileo)**?" He was saying, "Do you realize that you can only love me with your limited love?" That is why Peter was hurt. Peter realized the limitations of humanity without the Holy Spirit.

It is interesting to note that on the Day of Pentecost, when the Holy Spirit was poured out, that Peter was the first to act on this new empowerment of God's love. He preached the first New Testament sermon and 3,000 people were saved according to Acts 2.

Summary

When we are born again by God's Spirit we are literally empowered to overcome the limitations of mere humanity. We can love with God's love, walk in God's peace, take pleasure in God's joy, and minister to others with God's heart. The Holy Spirit made a real change in Peter because he understood that he was limited without God's presence in him and we can experience the same. When we realize that the Holy Spirit literally lives inside of us, we will be able to overcome our limitations and allow His love and His light to shine through us to make a difference in our environment every day!

*** Notes: Lesson #10 Weekly Reading ***

11. Encouragement – You Can Do It!
Romans 5:5;

> "All of this happens because God has given us the Holy Spirit, who fills our hearts with His love."

You Can Do It! It would be unrighteous of God to expect you to do something that He has not already equipped you to do. Whatever God expects you to do, He equips you to do. By the same token, whatever God equips you to do, He expects you to do. We come back to it because it is a reminder that God has given us His Holy Spirit. Romans 5 open with Paul teaching that we have been made acceptable to God by faith. Paul said, "…because of our Lord Jesus Christ, we live at peace with God." Paul goes on to teach us that Christ also introduced us to God's undeserved kindness and that this kindness makes us happy.

We feel an overwhelming joy when we come to Christ and our life is never the same. Paul also explains that life in Christ does not exonerate us from difficult situations. He teaches that learning to deal with difficult situations helps develop a passionate patience in us. This patience builds character and gives us hope. It is at this point that Paul teaches about the reality of the Holy Spirit.

The Holy Spirit comes to enable us to experience joy and overcome hardships. However, the latter part of this verse is the key. Paul teaches that part of the Holy Spirit's role is to *fill our hearts with God's love.*

The love of God was poured out in your heart when you were born again. God gave you His Spirit and His love so that you could do everything you have learned.

People are waiting to see Christians act like Christians. "For the earnest expectation of the creature waiteth for the manifestation of the sons of God" according to Romans 8:19.

People want to see a true difference in those that claim to be in Christ. When we truly walk in love they will see that difference in us and God will change their hearts through His love.

Summary

God has given you His Spirit and His love. You have everything you need to walk out what you have learned. As you make an effort to walk in love, you will allow God's light to shine through you and the hearts of others will be changed. No matter what you are facing and no matter how difficult your circumstances may be, don't allow anything to keep you from walking in God's love. You Can Do It!

*** Notes: Lesson #11 Weekly Reading ***

12. Operate With Your New Heart!
Ezekiel 11:19 AMP

"And I will give them one heart [a new heart] and I will put a new spirit within them; and I will take the stony [unnaturally hardened] heart out of their flesh, and will give them a heart of flesh [sensitive and responsive to the touch of their God]."

Ezekiel prophesied of a time where God would give His children a new heart; He would do this by giving them a new spirit. This new spirit would come in and replace their stony heart with a heart of flesh; a heart that is sensitive and responsive to the move and touch of God.

We see a similar prophecy in Ezekiel 36:25-27. Ezekiel prophesies, "I'll pour pure water over you and scrub you clean. I'll give you a new heart, put a new spirit in you." "I'll remove the stone heart from your body and replace it with a heart that's God-willed, not self-willed. I'll put my Spirit in you and make it possible for you to do what I tell you and live by my commands".

The difference in chapter 36 is that God explains the "spirit" He mentioned in chapter 11. Here, God, through Ezekiel, says that He will give us His Spirit. This is the promised Holy Spirit. This promise was fulfilled on the day of Pentecost and now we all receive God's Spirit when we are born-again.

Part of the role of the Holy Spirit in our lives is to remove our stony heart and replace it with a heart that is God-willed and not self-willed. Ezekiel 36 says that the Holy Spirit in us will enable us to live by the commands of God.

This means that the Holy Spirit can enable you to love those you cannot stand and be kind to those that treat you wrong. If you are willing to receive, you will be able to achieve through the power of the Holy Spirit.

Summary

God has given you the power to walk in His love, His will, and His way. He has given you this power through the Holy Spirit. It is no longer a question of whether or not you can; it is now a question of whether or not you will. If you submit your will to His will, you will see God's glorious power working through you and you will receive a transformation from a stony heart to a soft heart that is willing and wanting to please God. You have a new heart. Will you act like it today?

*** Notes: Lesson #12 Weekly Reading ***

13. You Prove You Love God By Loving Man
Matthew 22:34-40 NIV

"And the second is like it: 'Love your neighbor as yourself.' All the Laws and the Prophets hang on these two commandments."

I don't know if you remember the movie called "The Preacher's Wife" starring Denzel Washington and Whitney Houston. Near the end of the movie when the preacher was delivering his sermon and made this statement: "when we love people, we are loving God." By loving people, we are proving to God that we love Him. Some people claim to love God, but fail to love others. They claim that their relationship with God is personal and that it has nothing to do with how they treat others. Jesus taught on the end time judgment.

In Matthew 25; The following excerpts are from verses 31-46: "When the Son of Man comes in his glory with all of his angels, he will sit on his royal throne. People of all nations will be brought before him, and he will separate them... the king will say to those on his right... Come and receive the kingdom... When I was hungry, you gave me something to eat, and when I was thirsty, you gave me something to drink.

When I was a stranger, you welcomed me, and when I was naked, you gave me clothes to wear. When I was sick, you took care of me, and when I was in jail, you visited me." "... the people will ask, "When did we..."

The king will answer, "Whenever you did it for any of my people, no matter how unimportant they seemed, you did it for me." Then the king will say to those on his left, "Get away from me! You are under God's curse.

Go into the everlasting fire prepared for the devil and his angels! I was hungry, but you did not give me anything to eat, and I was thirsty, but you did not give me anything to drink.

I was a stranger, but you did not welcome me, and I was naked, but you did not give me any clothes to wear. I was sick and in jail, but you did not take care of me." Then Jesus said, "Those people will be punished forever. But the ones who pleased God will have eternal life."

Your love has to be more than lip service. There are many people that claim to be Christians, but Christianity is more than your parents' religion, or something you fill out on a form, or put on your ID tags; Christianity is living like Christ. The Bible has much to say about love, because love is the highest requirement of Christianity. People are turned away from God every day because of those that claim to be Christians, but never act like it. The world is waiting for the manifestation of true Christianity (Romans 8:19). Will they see it in you?

Summary

God expects you to prove your love for Him by sharing that love with others. During various holidays, make sure you do not get so engulfed in Santa Claus, Christmas trees, eggnog, and the Easter bunny, that you fail to remember the reason for the holiday. We are to celebrate the love of God manifested in His Son and show our love for God by being a blessing to someone else. Remember that whatever you do for others, no matter how unimportant they may seem, you are doing it for God!

*** Notes: Lesson #13 Weekly Reading ***

14. We are Bankrupt without Love!
1 Corinthians 13:1-3;

"Though I speak with the tongues of men and of angels, and have not charity, I am become as sounding brass, or a tinkling cymbal. And though I have the gift of prophecy, and understand all mysteries, and all knowledge; and though I have all faith, so that I could remove mountains, and have not charity, I am nothing. And though I bestow all my goods to feed the poor, and though I give my body to be burned, and have not charity, it profiteth me nothing."

In verse one Paul explains that eloquence without love is nothing but noise. There are many intellectually sound and verbally articulate people in the world; people that can stand and give a discourse about the Word of God without even knowing the God of the Word. These are people that talk about things they read, but not necessarily what they live. These people may be exalted by the world for their intellectual prowess and oratory skillfulness.

Paul lets us know that they are doing nothing for the Kingdom of God if their works are without love. In verse two, Paul lets us know that even if someone operated in divine revelation and special acts of faith, they would still be nothing without love. People don't care what you know until they know that you care. There are many theologians and biblically astute preachers that make poor pastors because they don't have a shepherd's heart.

When people are hurting and they need encouragement, they would much rather find a person that can share one scripture from their heart than a person that can share fifty scriptures from their head; or find a person that is motivated to pray for the sick because they have a genuine love for people and are not just "going through the motions" of praying.

In **verse three,** Paul explains that even outward acts of financial and human sacrifice are nothing if they are not performed in love. There are many people that support ministries or give to the poor with the wrong intentions. Although we should take advantage of tax law, tax write-offs should not be the motivation of our giving.

You can give without love, but you cannot truly love without giving.

Summary

We are bankrupt without love. We can be an usher at our church, teach a Sunday school class, financially support ministry, feed and clothe the poor, and pray for the sick; but it all means nothing if we are not doing everything in the love of God.

*** Notes: Lesson #14 Weekly Reading ***

15. The Most Excellent Way!
1 Corinthians 12:31;

"But earnestly desire the best gifts. And yet I show you a more excellent way."

Paul goes into great detail about spiritual gifts in the 12th chapter of his first letter to the church at Corinth. He explained to them that "There are different kinds of gifts, but the same Spirit… different kinds of service, but the same Lord… different kinds of working, but the same God works all of them in all men" (verses 4-6).

He went on to list nine spiritual gifts

Three gifts deal with the **"eyes" of God**: the Word of wisdom, the Word of knowledge, and prophecy. Three gifts deal with the **"hands" of God**: gifts of faith, gifts of healings, and the gift of working of miracles.

The final three gifts deal with the **"mind" of God**: the gift of discernment of spirits, the gift of speaking in different kinds of tongues, and the gift of interpretation of tongues. In the rest of the chapter, Paul goes on to explain the diversity of people and gifts that make up the body of Christ. What is very interesting is the way in which Paul closed the chapter. After going into such detail about spiritual gifts and the composition of the Body of Christ, the Holy Spirit through Paul said, "But eagerly desire the greater gifts. And now I will show you the most excellent way."

Paul uses this verse as what is commonly referred to as the "love chapter." I wanted you to know that Paul calls God's love, "the most excellent way."

Bigger than seeing through the "eyes" of God in prophecy; greater than operating with the "hands" of God in the working of miracles; and more important than receiving from the "mind" of God in the discernment of spirits; operating in God's love is the most excellent way.

Summary

Everything we attempt to do for God and His Kingdom comes down to a matter of intent. Many Christians seek spiritual gifts with the wrong intentions. They want to operate in some sort of spiritual power so that they can be exalted, but any motivation to do anything in the Kingdom of God must be rooted and grounded in the love of God. When you come to God with pure motives, God can use you to meet the needs of others, while still getting the glory Himself. When you come to God with impure motives, then you are simply attempting to make yourself look good.

Do you seek to glorify God with your life and in your living; or do you simply attempt to look good for yourself? This is an inward issue of motive and a clear issue of love. If you operate in the "most excellent way" today, God's blessing will enable you to accomplish everything you need to do, while still bringing glory to Him through your life! Are you ready to be blessed? Then walk in the love of God!

*** Notes: Lesson #15 Weekly Reading ***

Devotional on the Characteristics of Love
Introduction

The deeper I delve into God's Holy Word, the deeper is my understanding of what HIS love means for me as a believer. Everything that God does is a result of HIS love for us as HIS children. It is HIS unselfish love that gave us a Savior JESUS CHRIST the Son of the living God. Who shed HIS ever cleansing blood to redeem us. God is sitting on HIS Royal throne in Heaven with JESUS at HIS right side. However, HE has not left us alone; God also expresses HIS love for us by giving us a comforter through the Holy Spirit. The Holy Spirit is the power that dwells within every believer; giving us a direct line to God the Father who is the creator of all.

The Holy Spirit is our seal consecrating us as bonafide heirs of God. The Holy Spirit changes the way we view life as a whole. When we accepted JESUS CHRIST as our LORD and SAVIOR, believing that HE died on the Cross of Calvary, and was raised from the dead on the third day, has ascended to Heaven, and is seated at the right hand of God; we are given the seal The Holy Spirit. When we receive the Jesus as our Lord and Savior our lives will not be the same; we become new creatures in CHRIST. By learning to yield to Holy Spirit who is our helper there will be a positive change in our lives. The Holy Spirit is the one who causes the Love of God to be shed abroad in our hearts.

In the world people allow love to change how they view the world around them. They tend to smile more and are friendlier to others. If we were to use the movie "Pretty Woman" as an example of how the world views love, we could say that falling in love makes us better people.

The man "Edward" and the woman "Vivian" started out a little rough, but ending up falling in love with each other.

Once they began to fall in love, they allowed that love to change their lives for the better. Edward started to appreciate the simple things in life like walking in the park with no shoes, and taking time to enjoy life. Before falling in love, Edward would buy companies and destroy them, by selling off company products for profit. Then, after falling in love he was no longer self-seeking instead he became a kinder person who wanted to better companies.

Vivian got a chance to see life from a different point of view. She saw how bettering oneself through completing an education would give her a better life than the one she had. Vivian learned that love gives purpose to life and a sense of self worth. Love does not devalue people; it creates an appreciation for yourself and others. Just as the man and woman in the movie "Pretty Woman" changed their lives for the better after allowing themselves to fall in love, the same thing is to happen to us as believers when we receive the Jesus as our Lord and Savior.

When a person accept Jesus as their own personal lord and Savior the love of God is shed abroad in their heart by the Holy Spirit, and with the leading and teaching of the Holy Spirit the love of God will change the characteristics of our life.

As we continue to walk in love of God, the characteristics of God will be manifested in our lives. God's love will begin to affect every area of our lives.

We can become more connected to the things of God, No longer do we have to be in bondage doubting our purpose, being envious, hating and showing bitterness to our brothers and sisters. The love of God allows us to show our love for God by outwardly loving others and utilizing the Holy Spirit to help us walk in such a fashion. The love of God is residing on the inside of us, and enabling us to walk out the full manifestation of God's love as we cooperate with the Holy Spirit. The Love of God is shed aboard in our hearts and having HIS Word rooted and implanted in our hearts. We become lovers of God and have the ability to love as HE loves.

Vivian character changed once she fell in love giving her a new outlook in life. Naturally, when falling in love we want to change for the better. The same should be true from a spiritual perspective in our lives because the love of God in our hearts we desire to change our character how we talk, walk and live.

16. Love Endures Long
1 Corinthians 13:4;

"Love suffers long and is kind..." (1 Cor. 13:4)

Love does not give up easily. When you truly love someone you are able to look beyond their faults, flaws, and failures.

Let's look at the story of the prodigal son, (see Luke 15:11-31). This young man disrespected his father by asking for his inheritance early. Then he set off for a distant country and wasted the money on fast living. Having spent all his money and broken in spirit, he decided to go back home and ask his father for a job. He knew he had messed up and no longer considered himself a good son. He was willing to take the position of a hired servant. His father, on the other hand, was operating in love. He woke up every day expecting that his son would come home. One day, the son came home and while he was still a good ways off, the father saw him coming and was filled with compassion for him. The father was not filled with rage, resentment, or bitterness, but was filled with love for his son, the kind of love that "endured long.

He did not wait for his son to come to him; he ran out to his son, threw his arms around him, and kissed him. The son tried to explain that he was willing to be a hired servant, but the father ignored the foolish comments. Instead of saying, "I told you so," the father called his servants: "Quickly, bring the best robe and put it on my son. Put a ring on his finger and sandals on his feet. Bring the fattened calf and kill it. Let's have a feast and celebrate." (Luke 15:22, 23)

Summary

The love of God enables you to endure disappointments and mistakes by the ones that you love. When you operate in the love of God you are not quick to hold grudges, or focus on bad things. You are quick to forgive and move forward, choosing not to live in the past. Are you operating in the love of God?

Does your love endure long, or is it a love that operates only when others do what you want them to do? If that is the case, you might call it love, but it is not the love of God!

*** Notes: Lesson #16 Weekly Reading ***

17. Love Is Patient!
1 Corinthians 13:4-8;

"Love is patient." (1 Cor. 13:4)

God's Word Translation, God's love allows us to endure constant changes, while others complain every step of the way. It is easy to be nice to others when you are face-to-face with them, but then talk about them behind their back.

It is easy to say in public that our love for others endures long, but then privately despise them, because of their actions. One of the greatest truths I have learned about the love of God is that God's love is "**One-Sided!**" it never changes.

Paul describes God's incredible love for us in Romans 5:8: "But God demonstrates His own love toward us, in that while we were still sinners, Christ died for us."

How can we understand someone dying for us when we were sinners? God put his love on the line for us by offering his Son in sacrificial death because he loves us so much, and Jesus' death was the only way for us to be saved. God did not send Jesus to die for us because we were doing so much for him. It was not because we loved Him, worshipped Him, and gave Him all the glory in the earth. No! Even while we ignored, disrespected, and dishonored God; He loves us so much that He sent His son to die for our sins.

His love endures long and His love is patient. His love remains the same. His love is love. Even after we accept Jesus as Lord and Savior and attempt to live a life that is pleasing in God's sight, we make many mistakes.

What does God do when we make mistakes? Does He retract His love? Does He change the way He deals with us? Does He deal with us by using a ten foot pole? No! God's love never changes because His love is one-sided. He loves us, even when we fail to love Him back.

Summary

Patient love is consistent love. We are not operating in the love of God when we only love those that love us back and only love them while they are doing things that we approve of. God's love does not require a tit for a tat. God's love does not change when others do things we do not like. God's love empowers us to love others, even when you do not like what they are doing. God's love enables you to look beyond flaws and still love the flawed. God's love equips us with His consistency, even while the object of your love is inconsistent. God's love is one-sided, never changes. When you operate in one-sided love, you are able to consistently love others, even while they are living inconsistent lives!

*** Notes: Lesson #17 Weekly Reading ***

18. Love Is Kind!
1 Corinthians 13:4-8;

"Love is kind." (1 Cor. 13:4)

Webster's Dictionary defines the word "kind" as "being willing to do good for others, and to make them happy by granting their requests; having tenderness or goodness of nature; benevolent." If you read that definition again and you think of the ministry of Jesus you will quickly see that Jesus was kind. He was mindful to do good for others. He was inclined to meet their needs. He was good-natured and benevolent.

I mention that because Jesus is our example. As a matter of fact, we identify ourselves as Christians. The word "Christian" literally means "Like Christ." So if we claim to be like Him, should we make every effort to live like He lived, walk like He walked, and act like He acted? Paul also instructed us to be "…kind one to another, tenderhearted, forgiving one another" (Ephesians 4:32). A person who is kind is constantly looking for ways to be a blessing to others. They are literally seeking for opportunities to dispense good.

They get excited when an opportunity presents itself for them to meet the needs of another. What kind of testimony would the church have if a majority of Christians really walked in kindness?

What would happen if Christians walked in the love of God to the point where they were literally seeking to be a blessing to others every day? I can tell you that there is a great need for kindness today. The church needs to be a church of love and operate in kindness always.

People are looking for someone to be kind to them and God is looking for His children to meet needs.

God sends people our way and this is His method: He sets up divine appointments between His children and the hurting and the lost. He expects us to live what we have learned. God expects us to be willing to do good for others; especially at such a vital time as this.

Summary

People really do not care about the Christian screensaver you run on your computer, the Christian bumper sticker you display on your car, or the Christian music you play in your office. This is what they really want to know: is Christ living in you? They do not want to hear you talk about Christ; they want to see you live like Christ every day. Walking in love is the greatest witness. When you walk in the love of God and show kindness to others, people get a glimpse of Christ in the earth!

*** Notes: Lesson #18 Weekly Reading ***

19. Love Is Not Envious!
1 Corinthians 13:4-8;

"…love does not envy;" (1 Cor. 13:4)

Envy is a feeling of inadequacy and bitterness rooted in the perceived superiority of the possessions or qualities of another. Envy and jealousy stem from the fear of being superseded. We see a clear example of this in 1 Samuel, chapter 18. In chapter 17, young David conquered the uncircumcised Philistine (Goliath) with a slingshot and a stone.

Everyone was happy that Goliath was dead, even King Saul; because Goliath had been troubling Israel. In chapter 18, we see that the king's son, Jonathan, became instant friends with David. The king was so pleased with the outcome that he kept David with him from that moment on. David was quick to be awarded a high rank in the military and everything seemed to be going great. The people were happy, David was happy, Jonathan was happy, and the king was happy.

When the men were returning home after David had killed the Philistine, the women came out from all the towns of Israel to meet King Saul with singing and dancing; with joyful songs and with tambourines. They danced and sang, "Saul has slain his thousands and David his tens of thousands." This immediately bothered King Saul. He was very angry. He thought, "They have credited David with tens of thousands, but me with only thousands.

What more can he get but the kingdom?" The 9th verse makes it clear, "And from that time on Saul kept a jealous eye on David." Saul was the sitting king and David was a teenager, but Saul allowed himself to feel inadequate because of the praises the young man was receiving. That inadequacy led to bitterness and that bitterness led to several attempts to murder David.

Summary

When you operate in the love of God, you stand firm in the confidence of your own character and abilities; you have a healthy self-image; and you know that you have a special gift. Once you understand who you are, you can sincerely celebrate others' victories with a pure heart.

Looking at another's strengths and using that as motivation to get better is acceptable; but resenting them for their strengths is not. God's love instructs us to appreciate and not hate, and then we can celebrate.

*** *Notes: Lesson #19 Weekly Reading* ***

20. Love Is Not Boastful or Vainglorious!
1 Corinthians 13:4-8;

"…is not boastful or vainglorious," (1 Cor. 13:4 AMP)

To be boastful is to speak of one's self with excessive pride; having an excessively high opinion of oneself. Vainglory is unwarranted pride in one's accomplishments or qualities. In today's vernacular, this is basically being "full of oneself." There is a thin line between confidence and arrogance and even the best of us cross that line from time to time.

That is why it is important to constantly receive nourishment, guidance, and direction from the Word of God; in order that we might receive the correction we need to stay on the proper course. Pride is a weapon of our enemy. As a matter of fact, it is one of his three major weapons. According to 1 John 2:16, satan's "big three" are: 1) the lust of the flesh, 2) the lust of the eyes, and 3) the pride of life. Also, in Proverbs 16:18, Solomon said, "Pride goes before destruction… ".

What happened to satan? He operated in pride and was kicked out of heaven as described in the book of Isaiah: "Satan said, "I will ascend to heaven; I will raise my throne above the stars of God; I will sit enthroned on the mount of assembly, on the utmost heights of the sacred mountain.

I will ascend above the tops of the clouds; I will make myself like the Most High" (Isaiah 14:13, 14). What do you see in those two verses? Satan had an excessively high opinion of himself and it got him in trouble.

Summary

You should appreciate everything the Lord has enabled you to do, but you don't have to go around telling everyone about it. If you are good at what you do, allow others to say how good you are. You don't need to boast on yourself. When Jesus was questioned by the high priest on whether or not he was the Son of God, Jesus answered, "That is what you say..." (Matthew 26:63, 64);

In other words, Jesus was saying, "I do not need to go around saying who I am and what I can do, I will allow you to do it for me." We should follow Jesus' example. If you are truly talented and a hard worker, then simply continue to be faithful to do your best and God will open doors for you. Solomon, was the richest man in the world and he said that your gift "will make room for you and bring you before great men" (Proverbs 18:16). So walk in love, remain humble, and God will exalt you!

*** Notes: Lesson #20 Weekly Reading ***

21. Love Does Not Display Itself Haughtily
1st Corinthians 13:4-8;

"...does not display itself haughtily." (1 Cor. 13:4 AMP)

To be haughty is to be condescendingly proud or to believe others to be inferior. The text says that love does not display itself to be that way. In other words, people that walk in the love of God do not conduct themselves in such a manner that they put others down and cause them to feel inferior.

Have you ever met a person that seemed to talk down to everyone? People that talk down to others often cause bitterness; resentment, and offense; and these are definitely not the goals of Christianity

People that operate in haughtiness are people that cause harm and not help. They lower the self-esteem of others, instead of helping to raise it. They tear down rather than build up. They put down rather than encourage. There are haughty people in this world, but haughtiness should not be an identifying characteristic of a Christian. When you say you are a Christian and you declare that God Himself lives inside of you, then there ought to be some sort of evidence of His presence.

The greatest evidence is walking in His love. When you walk in His love, you seek to be a blessing and not a burden, You seek to build up and not tear down, You seek to walk in peace and not offense, You seek to make others feel superior and not inferior.

Summary

You must be considerate when dealing with others. The old adage, "sticks and stones may break my bones, but words will never hurt me" is simply not true. Words can hurt. When you look and talk down to people you can actually help destroy their dreams, instead of encouraging them to pursue their dreams and become what God has destined for them to become. Be cognizant, today, of how you talk to and deal with people.

When dealing with a private or a general, a pauper or a President, your subordinate or your superior; always remember to treat them as God would have you to treat them and to be a blessing and not a burden!

*** Notes: Lesson #21 Weekly Reading ***

22. Love Is Not Conceited
1 Corinthians 13:4-8;

"It is not conceited (arrogant and inflated with pride);"
(1 Corinthians. 13:5 AMP)

To be conceited is to have or display a sense of overbearing self-worth or self-importance. This is a character trait that can literally cause God's favor to cease from operating in your life. Peter told us that God resists the proud, but gives grace to the humble (1 Peter 5:5). You don't want to be on the other side of God's resistance. We see an example of this in 1st Samuel, chapter 15.

The Lord spoke to King Saul through the Prophet Samuel and said, "I am the one the Lord sent to anoint you king over his people Israel; so listen now to the message from the Lord. This is what the Lord Almighty says: 'I will punish the Amalekites... Now go, attack the Amalekites and totally destroy everything that belongs to them. Do not spare them... "(Verses 1-3);

Later on in the text we see that Saul partially obeyed. Saul attacked the Amalekites and had the people killed, but he decided to take the King of the Amalekites (Agag) alive. He was also supposed to kill the animals, but he decided to keep the best of the sheep and cattle, supposedly to offer up a sacrifice to God. God was not pleased with this at all.

Partial obedience is disobedience. God sent Samuel to express His displeasure with the King. In verse 17, we see to what God attributed the disobedience.

The Message Bible says, "When you started out in this, you were nothing – and you knew it." The King James Version says, "When thou was little in thine own sight..." What was the problem? Saul had gotten to the point where his self-importance as King caused him to disobey the God that he was supposed to be serving with the position in the first place. Let's learn from his mistake and not repeat it.

Summary

God can bless us and we should expect Him to. We should expect to go higher and further every day. We should pray for and believe that God's favor will be upon our lives. We should never get to the point where we are so "big" in our own eyes that we fail to honor the God that is the origin of our blessings; nor should we ever have a sense of overbearing self-importance.

I do agree that Christians should never have low self-esteem, and love keeps it all in balance. Love keeps us from getting the "big head." Love keeps us rooted. Love enables us to appreciate the blessings that God has given to us, to the point where we never dishonor God, nor do we dishonor man!

*** Notes: Lesson #22 Weekly Reading ***

23. Love Is Not Rude
1 Corinthians 13:4-8;

"…it is not rude (unmannerly)…" (1 Cor. 13:5 AMP)

The modern day translations for the word "rude" tell us that being rude is to act in an offensive manner; to be abruptly and unpleasantly forceful; to be discourteous, coarse, or vulgar. In the original language of our text, to be rude means to become easily provoked or irritated. Love is not these things.

Love is not offensive towards others, but rather makes every effort to avoid offense. Jesus said, "Woe to that man by whom the offence cometh." (Matthew 18:7). Love is not easily irritated, but rather has a high tolerance for people. Love does not force its way upon others, especially when it comes to personal beliefs. I preach that every Christian should know what they believe, that they should remain firm in their beliefs, and that they should be led of the Holy Spirit to share the light of the gospel with a dark, dying, and decaying world.

The need for evangelism, however, is not a license for offense. I have met many Christians who commonly offend others under the guise of evangelism. It is important that we share the truth of the gospel message, but you can do so in such a way as to avoid offense. You can force your beliefs upon someone, cause an argument, and maybe even win the argument; but winning the argument does not equal winning a soul. If you win the argument, but they leave offended, ministry has not taken place.

Love is not rude. The Message Bible says that it "doesn't fly off the handle." Love does not seek to offend, but rather to reconcile. Love does not seek to cause offense, but rather to share with others while operating in harmony. Love seeks to meet needs without causing problems.

Summary

Spirituality is not a license to be rude or mean-spirited towards others. God wants you to draw others towards Him, not drive them away. God wants you to meet the needs of others, but to do so in such a way as to avoid offense. When people think of you they should think of the love of God.

Take a moment to allow His Word to be a mirror for you before you face this day. Look in the mirror and ask yourself if you like what you see. Are you rude towards others? Are you easily provoked or irritated?

Do you cause others to be offended? If so, then **repent** this morning and ask God to allow His love and His light to be perfected in you this day and this week.

*** Notes: Lesson #23 Weekly Reading ***

24. Love Does Not Act Unbecomingly
1 Corinthians 13:4-8;

"...and does not act unbecomingly." (1 Cor. 13:5 AMP)

To act unbecomingly simply means to be inappropriate; to fail to comply with the standards implied by one's character or position. I am a pastor and a common term used in ministry is "conduct unbecoming" of a pastor or minister. This term is used when a person's actions do not correspond with their rank. In other words, there is a level of expectation tied to every rank or position in the Body of Christ; the higher the rank, the greater the expectation. The implied expectations of someone operating in one of the fivefold office gifts are much greater than the implied expectations on a Christian layperson, and rightly so. A person operating in one of the fivefold office gifts may have twenty to thirty years of experience, in most cases, and will, therefore, be expected to make tactical, personal, and moral decisions that reflect that experience. Anything less is conduct that is unbecoming.

You may be wondering what this has to do with the Body of Christ. Well, the same principle applies. The text says that love does not act unbecomingly. We have covered the fact that God's love was poured out in our hearts when we were born-again (Romans 5:5). We also learned that His love was actually Himself, because God is love according to 1 John 4:8; that Jesus commanded us to love according to John 13:34; and that Jesus stated that love would be the identifying characteristic of His disciples (verse 35). Paul explained to us that love is the "most excellent way" according to 1 Corinthians 12:31; and that we are bankrupt without it.

We must also never forget that Jesus lived His life as the ultimate example for us. He showed us what "right" looks like. He lived the standard.

While Jesus was hanging on Calvary's cross, with nails in His hands and feet, after being unjustly tried and beaten, He looked down at the people and said, "Father, forgive them; for they know not what they do." What was Jesus doing? He was operating in love!

Summary

Jesus was and is our standard. The standard has been set for Christian living. We act unbecomingly when we fail to comply with the standards implied by our position in the Body of Christ. Remember, your consideration should be based on whether or not you are operating in the love of God.

*** Notes: Lesson #24 Weekly Reading ***

25. Love Does Not Insist On Its Own Way
1 Corinthians 13:4-8;

"… does not insist on its own rights or its own way,.."
(1 Corinthians 13:5 AMP)

There is a degree of compromise woven into most relationships. It is unrealistic and improbable to think that you will walk through life without having differences of opinions with others. Learning to deal with disagreements is healthy and necessary particularly in the Body of Christ and life in general. From the time little boys and little girls are taught to "play nice" on the playground to the time where grown men and women pass from the temporal to the eternal, compromise is required.

Marriage, family, friendship, and even co-worker relationships require some level of compromise when dealing with disagreements. A compromise is a settlement of differences in which each side makes concessions. It is an acknowledgement of the validity of someone's opinion or position. This is a healthy reality because it helps keep us grounded in the fact that we are not always right. Even in the cases where we believe strongly that we are right, we might be led of God to concede on some issues, in order that we might keep the peace in our marriage, friendships, and workplace.

Why is this a big deal? Because persons who insist on their own rights and their own way all the time consistently cause offense, Remember that characteristic #3 was kindness.

We have learned that kindness is being mindful to do good to others, seeking for ways to make others happy. When we insist on our own way, we are doing the exact opposite.

Instead of causing others to be blessed, persons who insist on their own way all the time provoke resentment, bitterness, and anger in others. This is just simply not the goal of Christianity.

Summary

Others are sometimes right and at times when they are not completely right, love seeks for ways to settle differences by allowing both sides to make concessions.

When one person in a relationship consistently insists on their own way, it leads to domination; domination leads to frustration; and frustration often ends in dissatisfaction and resentment. This should not be your goal as a Christian. Seek to be a blessing and not a burden today and remember that you don't always have to get your way!

*** Notes: Lesson #25 Weekly Reading ***

26. Love Is Not Self-seeking!
1 Corinthians 13:4-8;

"…for it is not self-seeking;" (1 Cor 13:5 AMP)

To be self-seeking is to be overly concerned with your own interests, desires, or needs. Being passionate and determined for personal advancement is not a bad thing, but people who are self-seeking are passionate about their personal advancement, even if it comes at the cost of others. Self seeking people are simply selfish. The root word for selfish is "self." Selfish people put their desires above everyone else's and neglect others in their pursuit of personal satisfaction.

This is definitely not a characteristic of a person who is walking in the love of God. There are many descriptions in the Bible of what God is "like," but I have only found two declarations of what God literally "is." 1 John 1:5 says that God is light. 1 John 4:8 says that God is love. God is like many things, but it is clear that He is both light and love. The opposite of light is darkness. There are many scriptures that support the fact that God wants us to "walk in the light" and not the darkness.

Likewise, the opposite of love is selfishness. There are many scriptures (today's text included) that support the fact that God does not want us to be selfish. I have often stated that you can give without loving, but you cannot truly love without giving. Love requires you to take into consideration the needs, cares and concerns of others.

Summary

You should strive to be your best, endeavor to succeed in everything God allows you to do, and seek excellence in every area of your life; but you should not do it while neglecting and stepping on or over other people.

God does not want to know how many times you made it up the mountain of success; He wants to know how many people you were able to take with you. People that are really good are people who are able to help other people become better! Are you one of those people or are you so concerned with yourself that you neglect others? God wants you to be a blessing, not a burden. Are you being that blessing by empowering others to be better or are you being a burden by succeeding at the cost of others?

*** Notes: Lesson #26 Weekly Reading ***

27. Love Is Not Touchy or Resentful
1 Corinthians 13:4-8;

"…it is not touchy or fretful or resentful;"
(1 Corinthians 13:5 AMP)

A touchy person is a person that tends to take offense for the slightest reason, being oversensitive. This person will require special tactics when you are dealing with them. Any insignificant event may cause them to become extremely angry. A fretful person is inclined to be displeased or troubled. This person is looking for things to go wrong and looking for ways to be upset.

A resentful person is a person that keeps a persistent ill will towards those that have wronged them. Even after an apology has been rendered, a resentful person will harbor ill feelings for a long time. Have you ever met a person like this? I am sure you have. Talking with a touchy person is like walking into a land mine. You may say something like, "I like your shoes; where did you get them?" And they might reply, "Why do you want to know where I got my shoes? I cannot stand copycats! I am tired of people trying to be like me! Why can't you just find your own shoes?" This is an example of how a fretful person would act.

Finally, a resentful person does not only get upset, but they hold on to inner anger for a long time. We have all encountered resentful people, but this is definitely not God's desire for His children. As children of God, we should be children of love and children of light. We must rule our emotions and not allow our emotions to rule us.

I have met many believers in the Body of Christ that allow their emotions to rule them to the point where they are living their lives on an emotional roller coaster.

Summary

God wants you to live a strong, stable, and satisfied life; but this type of life will elude you if you allow yourself to be ruled by your emotions. Emotional people are touchy, fretful and resentful. Emotional people are unstable, unbalanced and insecure. Are you an emotional person that is easily offended or are you a stable person that possesses the ability to remain the same in spite of circumstances?

*** Notes: Lesson #27 Weekly Reading ***

28. Love Is Not Resentful
1 Corinthians 13:4-8;

"...it takes no account of the evil done to it [it pays no attention to a suffered wrong]." (1 Cor. 13:6 AMP)

Let's look at two other translations. This portion of the verse is translated "thinketh no evil" in the King James Version; "does not keep a record of wrongs" in the Good News Bible.

I remember commercials about attending college and the message at the end of these commercials was, "A mind is a terrible thing to waste." Unfortunately, many Christians waste valuable brain power on the wrong things; spending a great deal of time nursing and rehearsing the wrong done to them. The Bible clearly teaches us to meditate on the Word of God day and night. Meditation is powerful. The word "meditate" used in Joshua 1:8 and Psalm 1:3 means more than just to think about; it also means to mutter. We are to constantly think about the Word of God, and we should also constantly speak the Word of God. There is a level of faith that is activated when we think and speak the Word of God according to Romans 10:9, 10.

When we consistently think (believe) and speak a portion of scripture, we activate that scripture in our lives. This is the power of biblical meditation. If you replay evil done to you over and over in your mind, you will find yourself talking about it as well.

Jesus taught us that our mouth will speak out of the overflow of our heart according to Matthew 12:34.

So, if we consistently think about the wrongs done to us, we will begin to speak about them which activates a negative force and not a positive force over our lives.

Not only is this destructive for all parties involved, but it is not God's will. When you think on evil things it will lead to physical maladies like high blood pressure, stress, tension, etc...; and more importantly, it hinders spiritual growth. Unforgiveness is what I call a "blessing blocker". This will hinder God's favor from flowing upon our lives.

Summary

You should not waste the power of your mind or your mouth on negative things. The love of God meditates on the Word of God day and night. The love of God forgives and moves forward. The love of God doesn't keep good records of bad things. The love of God prays for those that do us wrong. Are you ready to forgive and walk in the love of God this day? If so, you will experience spiritual and physical blessing!

*** Notes: Lesson #28 Weekly Reading ***

29. Love Does Not Rejoice at Injustice!
1 Corinthians 13:4-8;

"…It does not rejoice at Injustice and Unrighteousness…" (1 Corinthians 13:6 AMP)

To rejoice, is to experience joy; an intense feeling of happiness. Love does not break out into this intense feeling of happiness over the misfortune of another. Have you ever met someone who loved to see others fail or hurt? These people are simply not walking in the love of God. Christians should not take the opportunity to celebrate the fact that others are going through tough times. As a matter of fact, we should sympathize with them and show compassion towards those who are "going through." We should seek to be a blessing and not a burden.

Jesus had an intense meeting with a family that he loved in John, chapter 11. Mary and Martha were crying because their brother (Lazarus) was dead and he had been dead for four days. They sent word to Jesus while Lazarus was still alive. When Jesus got there, He encountered a hurting family because Lazarus was dead. What did He do when He met with the family that was grieving?

What did He do when He saw their tears? Did He break out into a dance and celebrate the fact that they were hurting? Of course not! He was sorrowful with them, and then He raised Lazarus from the dead.

The Bible says, "Jesus wept" according to John 11:35. He cried with them. He shared their feelings. He shared their pain. Why? Because He was operating in the love of God.

Paul said, "A body is made up of many parts, and each of them has its own use. That is how it is with us.

There are many of us, but we each are part of the body of Christ, as well as part of one another" (Romans 12:4, 5).

If one part of our body hurts, we will eventually hurt all over. If one part of our body is honored, the whole body will be happy" according to 1 Corinthians 12:26. And He also said, "Rejoice with those who rejoice [sharing others' joy], and weep with those who weep [sharing others' grief]" (Romans 12:15 AMP).

It is clear that the Holy Spirit, through Paul, taught us to care for one another. We are all members of the Body of Christ and we should share in each others' disappointments and successes; but the love of God is not confined to just other Christians. It would be a poor witness if we only love those who love the name of Jesus. Our light shines best in darkness. We must allow the love and the light of God to reach those who are hurting and do not know God so that they will come into the saving knowledge of Jesus Christ!

Summary

You must be considerate. Celebrate with others when they are celebrating, but also be compassionate towards those who are hurting. We should not take pleasure in other's pain; but rather seek to be a blessing when they are down.

*** Notes: Lesson #29 Weekly Reading ***

30. Love Rejoices When Right and True Prevail!
1 Corinthians 13:4-8;

"...but rejoices when right and truth prevail."
(1 Corinthians 13:6 AMP)

Webster's dictionary says that truth is 'that which is considered to be the supreme reality and to have the ultimate meaning and value of existence and righteousness, among other things, is applied to God, the perfection of His nature."

Moreover the Bible states that God is a God of truth according to Deuteronomy 32:4, Jesus was full of truth according to John 1:14, the Holy Spirit is the Spirit of truth according to John 14:17, who guides us into all truth according to John 16:13, the Word of God is truth according to Daniel 10:21, and John 17:17. God made Jesus to be sin for us so that we might be made righteous according to 2 Corinthians 5:21.

God expects us to be different! If we are not operating in light and truth, then we are operating in deception and darkness and rejoicing in ungodly things. Paul explained it well when he said that we were children of disobedience and by nature, children of wrath according to Ephesians 2:2, 3. Prior to salvation, we all operated as agents of satan's kingdom. Jesus explained that there is no truth in him.

Jesus also said, "...There is nothing truthful about satan. satan speaks on his own, and everything he says is a lie. Not only is he a liar, but he is also the father of all lies" according to John 8:44.

Summary

Christians should rejoice in and about the things of God. You should not rejoice when darkness is in operation. When you see satan having his way with people, it is not the time to laugh at them or to take pleasure in their pain, but rather pray for them and lead them into the light. When we become Christians, we must realize and know that we have been changed.

We should not take pleasure in watching television shows, plays, movies, etc. that are degrading and focus on the chaos of the world, but we should take pleasure in things that are true, just, honest, honorable, and right.

*** Notes: Lesson #30 Weekly Reading ***

31. Love Bears Up Under Anything and Everything that Comes
1 Corinthians 13:4-8;

"Love bears up under anything and everything that comes…" (1 Cor. 13:7 AMP)

The word translated as "bears up" in this text means to protect, preserve, cover, keep secret, hide, conceal. It also means to carry in the mind, to carry from one place to another; transport. We have learned that love is kind, and empowers us to do good for others. We have learned through many of the characteristics of love that this tendency to dispense good should not be shaken by temporary circumstance.

We all make mistakes and love enables us to look beyond the mistakes and continue to love the mistaken. Solomon said it this way, "Hatred stirs up trouble; love overlooks the wrongs that others do" (Proverbs 10:12). Peter also explained it by saying, "Above all things have intense and unfailing love for one another, for love covers a multitude of sins [forgives and disregards the offenses of others]" (1 Peter 4:8 AMP).

To bear up under our brothers and sisters literally means to be able and willing to carry their burdens. People should be able to come to us and share their heart and their faults without a concern that we will broadcast their faults to the world. Love is mindful to hide or conceal the faults and imperfections of others.

Love does not transmit or give undue publicity to the flaws and faults of others. People should know that we have the ability to carry their issues without ever having to reveal them.

Summary

We all makes mistakes and we all need someone to confide in and to share our heart and issues with. It also means that you must develop a sense of care and concern for people, to the point where you will not share openly what they have shared with you privately. As we bear up one another's burdens, we will find ourselves helping one another by being the man or woman of God that God has intended for us to be.

*** Notes: Lesson #31 Weekly Reading ***

32. Love is Ever Ready To Believe the Best of Every Person
1 Corinthians 13:4-8;

"…is ever ready to believe the best of every person…" (1 Corinthians 13:7 AMP)

Love is ever ready to believe the best of every person. This is a big one. I have dealt with many people who consistently believe the worst of people. Love is always ready to believe the best, no matter what. However, this does not mean that God wants you to be gullible. It does not mean that the person walking in the influence of God's love is under some type of mystical spell that makes them naïve; where they fail to see the difference between right and wrong; or they are prone to believe a falsehood as the truth; or that they do not make the effort to investigate the truth.

What I mean is that a person walking in the love of God will give the benefit of the doubt; always ready to believe the best of every person; tends to believe that others are acting upon good motives. Love produces this type of positive expectation because it rejoices in the happiness and goodness of others and refuses to believe the contrary except on irrefutable evidence. To put it another way, love has faith in men. Love wants to believe that people are good and not evil. Love wants to believe the best and not the worst.

I have met many that have lost faith in people. They have been hurt so many times that now they refuse to allow others to get close to them and they expect the worst from people.

These types of people close themselves down towards others and build up walls of resentment, bitterness, and pain. Love refuses to allow the actions of others to influence our actions towards the masses.

Summary

Love empowers us to forgive those that have hurt us. Love allows us to continue to expect the best out of people. Have you been hurt in the past?

Please don't allow yourself to expect the worst from the world because of the hurt caused by a few. There are people in this world that are here to bless you and others here for you to bless. If you have the wrong attitude you might miss both opportunities!

*** Notes: Lesson #32 Weekly Reading ***

33. Love Its Hopes are Fadeless under all Circumstances
1 Corinthians 13:4-8;

> "…its hopes are fadeless under all circumstances…"
> (1 Corinthians13:7 AMP)

To hope is to look forward to with a confident expectation. Hope desires the best outcome possible. Hope expects a positive result. In this context, it is dealing with relationships with other people. Characteristic 17 stated that love is ever ready to believe the best of every person. Hope now takes it a step further.

When there is no place left for believing good of a person, love comes in with its hope. Even when it is clear that a person has done wrong, love still confidently expects that they will do better. Love loves them in spite of their faults and anticipates a "turn around" in the heart of the transgressor, and believes God for a complete (physical, social, mental, and spiritual) restoration.

No matter how hopeless someone may seem, love hopes for the best for them and their situation. This is part of the resilient character of God's love. Love will hold on to this "confident expectation" for years if need be. I know a few men and women who have expectantly waited on their spouses to make a "turn around" for years.

Likewise, I know some people who have endured a great deal with their children, but they never gave up hope, even when it was clear that the situation looked grim and the possibilities were limited.

God's love is able to look beyond problems and see promises; look beyond obstacles and see opportunities and look beyond flaws and failures by faith. Why? Because love's hopes are fadeless under all circumstances!

Summary

God's love "in" you will enable you to hope beyond natural hope. The bible says that Abraham "against hope believed in hope" according to Romans 4:18; because he was standing on the Word of God. His situation was beyond natural hope, but he still believed and God eventually turned his situation around. Likewise, you may have a situation with a loved one that seems hopeless.

The love of God "in" you can enable you to look beyond hopelessness and trust God who can turn hopeless situations around. Do you love them enough not to give up hope? Keep on believing for their "turn around." Operate in fadeless hope and eternal expectation!

*** Notes: Lesson #33 Weekly Reading ***

34. Love Endures Everything Weakening
1 Corinthians 13:4-8;

"...and it endures everything [without weakening]." (1 Corinthians 13:7 AMP)

Paul said, "Don't be so naive and self-confident. You're not exempt. You could fall flat on your face as easily as anyone else. Forget about self-confidence; it's useless. Cultivate God-confidence. No test or temptation that comes your way is beyond the course of what others have had to face. All you need to remember is that God will never let you down; he'll never let you be pushed past your limit; he'll always be there to help you come through it." Accord to 1 Corinthians 10:12, 13; not only will God help you come through it, but love enables you to remain the same while you are coming through.

Love endures persecutions and mistreatment from open enemies and professed friends; and still continues to love. Love endures people talking about you behind your back and lying to you to your face; and still continues to love. Love endures disappointments from loved ones and outright attacks from adversaries; and still continues to love.

This does not mean that love never gets upset or that love never dislikes the actions of others, but what it does mean is that love can stand in the midst of unlikable and unpleasant circumstances and still operate in our lives. God is love and He can endure anything.

This same God, who is love, lives inside of us. The issue now is whether or not we will allow God's consistent love to operate in our lives.

Summary

You don't have to like everything and everyone, but you still are commanded to love. It also means that this love is not a passive and wavering emotion, but rather a consistent and stable force that can operate in our lives. Are you ready to allow the force of consistent love to transform you into the image and the likeness of Christ? If so, there is nothing that God will withhold from you!

*** **Notes: Lesson #34 Weekly Reading** ***

35. Love Never Fails
1 Corinthians 13:4-8;

"Love never fails never fades out or becomes obsolete or comes to an end;" 1 Corinthians 13:8

If something has been superseded, then it has been set aside, displaced, replaced, or removed; all because the issue/item has become obsolete, inferior, or antiquated. This gives us a better understanding of our text. The text connotes that the gifts of prophecy and tongues have had and continue to have their role in the Kingdom of God, but there will come a time when they will be obsolete. When Jesus returns (ultimately) or when a believer dies (more directly) the role of prophecy and tongues ceases; but love will continue to operate, because God is love according to 1 John 4:8; Love is an eternal requirement so we might as well come to grips with it.

Love will never lose its relevancy, never become outdated, and never be replaced by some "higher" characteristic. Most importantly, love will never become inferior to anything else. Love is God's highest calling. You cannot get around it, over it, or under it. Remember what Paul said at the beginning of 1Corinthians, chapter 13, "If I speak with human eloquence and angelic ecstasy but do not love, I am nothing but the creaking of a rusty gate. If I speak God's Word with power, revealing all his mysteries and making everything plain as day, and if I have faith that says to a mountain, "Jump," and it jumps, but I do not love, I am nothing.

If I give everything I own to the poor and even go to the stake to be burned as a martyr, but I do not love, I have gotten nowhere. So, no matter what I say, what I believe, and what I do, I am bankrupt without love."

Summary

God requires us to operate in love today and forever. There will be no hatred in heaven, so we might as well prepare ourselves now (in time) for eternity.

Create a checklist of these 20 characteristics of love and seek to perfect them in your life. If you want to know if you are growing in Christ, then simply measure whether or not you are growing in love. You can go to church every Sunday morning and Wednesday night; you can participate in programs and ministries; you can get accolades for your dedication to the Pastor and the vision; but if you are not growing in love you are not growing in God!

*** Notes: Lesson #35 Weekly Reading ***

DEVOTIONAL ON The Action of Love
Introduction

Live Carefully - Several years ago, a preacher from out of state accepted a call to a church in Houston, Texas. Some weeks after he arrived, he had an occasion to ride the bus from his home to the downtown area. When he sat down, he discovered that the driver had accidentally given him a quarter too much change. As he considered what to do, he thought to himself, "You'd better give the quarter back. It would be wrong to keep it." Then he thought, "Oh, forget it, it's only a quarter. Who would worry about this little amount? Anyway, the bus company gets too much fare; they will never miss it. Accept it as a gift from God and keep quiet."

When his stop came, he paused shortly at the door, and then he handed the quarter to the driver and said, "Here, you gave me too much change." The driver, with a smile, replied, "Aren't you the new preacher in town? I have been thinking a lot lately about going somewhere to worship. I just wanted to see what you would do if I gave you too much change. I'll see you at church on Sunday." When the preacher stepped off the bus, he literally grabbed the nearest light pole, held on, and said, "Oh God, I almost sold your Son for a quarter." Our lives are the only Bible some people will ever read. This is a scary example of how much people watch us as Christians and will put us to the test! Always be on guard and remember. You carry the name of Christ on your shoulders when you call yourself "Christian." Watch your thoughts; they become words.

Watch your words; they become actions. Watch your actions; they become habits. Watch your habits; they become character. Watch your character; it becomes your destiny

36. Love Your Enemies!
Luke 6:27;

"To you who are ready for the truth, I say this: Love your Enemies, Let them bring out the best in you, not the worst."

In Luke 6, Jesus was being followed by a great number of disciples. He broke away from the crowd and spent all night praying for direction. The next morning He chose the 12 Apostles. He went on to minister to the crowd, healing the sick and casting out demons.

He then began to teach them (verses 20-26). It was after this teaching that Jesus said, "To you who are ready for the truth, I say this: Love your enemies..." It was as if Jesus was saying, "Ok, you guys have seen me minister to the needs of people and heard me teach principles of the Kingdom of God; but if you think you are ready for the next level, you must start by operating in the love of God." Jesus made it clear from the beginning that Godly love extends beyond human love. Human love loves those that love them back. Human love loves those that are easy to love. Human love is contingent upon circumstances being right, but the love of God empowers us to extend beyond the limitations of human love and to love those that we would never love otherwise. The word "action" means the process of doing or performing something. Love is more than just thinking. Love is more than just dreaming. God's love in us manifests itself in the earth in a tangible form. We must "act out" the love that we profess to possess.

Webster says that an enemy is one who feels hatred toward, intends injury to, or opposes the interests of another; a foe.

Jesus had many enemies while He walked the earth, but their actions against Him and His ministry never stopped Jesus from loving those flaws and all.

Summary

There will always be people who do not like you and there may even be some that are outright against you; but do not allow your dislike for the actions of a person to lead to a hatred for the person. Hate the sin, but love the sinner. Dislike the negative things acted out towards you, but ask God to empower you to still love the person. Love them enough to earnestly pray for them. Love them enough to want to see God's best for them.

I know this is a hard thing – believe me, I understand – but when you truly love those that are coming against you, you find yourself being transformed into the true image and likeness of Christ. You've been learning about what love is, are you ready to be an example of God's love in action?

*** Notes: Lesson #36 Weekly Reading ***

37. Overcome Evil With Good!
Luke 6:27;

"To you who are ready for the truth, I say this: Love your enemies. Let them bring out the best in you, not the worst."

Overcome evil with good. This is based on the latter part of our scripture. Jesus said, "Let them bring out the best in you, not the worst." A good example of this is found in Matthew, chapter 14. John the Baptist got in trouble because he spoke out about a situation that he judged to be immoral. This is something that could have easily been a part of today's tabloids. Phillip was the brother of Herod and was married to Herodias, the granddaughter of Herod the Great Josephus.

According to a first century scholar, this marriage took place as a result of a trip to Rome where two married couples decided to swap spouses. To make matters worse, not only did Phillip take Herodias to be his wife, after she was the wife of another, but they were also related. John the Baptist publicly spoke out against this and became a marked man. Soon, Herod had John the Baptist arrested for speaking out against his brother.

One night Herod's family threw him a big birthday party. His niece, Herodias' daughter, was there and she danced for her uncle. He was so pleased that he made the mistake of promising, with an oath, to give her whatever she asked.

Her mother jumped on the opportunity and pushed her to ask for the death of John the Baptist. The girl caved in and said, "Give me here on a platter the head of John the Baptist" (verse 8).

The king did not want to do it, but he was obligated by his word. So John the Baptist was beheaded in prison and his head was brought to the girl on a platter.

When Jesus found out what happened, He privately withdrew by boat to a solitary place. John the Baptist was not just a prophet, but he was also Jesus' cousin. I am sure that the matter by which he died made it worse. If John had died for preaching the gospel it would have been a different story; but John died as a result of a birthday party prank and I am sure that Jesus felt the pain of it.

So how would love react?

Would love put a curse on Herod? Would love go to Herod's house and pick a fight? Would love call angels down to destroy Herod's entire family? NO! Love knew that this was an attack from the kingdom of darkness, attempting to destroy the work of God; so love would counterattack the kingdom of darkness and destroy the works of satan. When Jesus' boat **reached** the other side, there was a huge crowd waiting on Him and many of them were sick. Jesus got out of the boat, was moved with compassion, and He healed their sick (verse 14).

Summary

There is an overwhelming satisfaction that comes from firing back at evil with good. Jesus could have done many things, but He chose to be a blessing and not a curse. He chose to do good and not evil. He chose to overcome evil with good.

When something bad happens to you or your family, what will you do? Will you seek to retaliate with evil or will you overcome evil with good?

*** Notes: Lesson #37 Weekly Reading ***

38. Pray For Those That Give You a Hard Time!
Luke 6:28;

> "When someone gives you a hard time, respond with the energies of prayer for that person."

He was falsely accused, run through bootleg trails, convicted without one witness, slapped in the face, spat on, mocked, ridiculed, beaten, and then caused to hang on a beam between two real criminals; all three of them with nails driven through their hands and feet. Moreover, to add insult to injury, they drove a crown of thorns into his skull and put a sign over His head that read, "THIS IS THE KING OF THE JEWS." How would love respond to this treatment? Jesus could have called down a legion of angels to destroy them all, but Jesus looked beyond their actions and said, "Father, forgive them, for they do not know what they are doing" (Luke 23:34).

Now, you might say, "this was all part of prophecy and Jesus forgave them because it had to happen." I come back and say that Jesus forgave them and prayed for them because that is what love does. Our scripture reference clearly states that we should pray for those that give us a hard time. Still, there are those who would argue the point. They could mention that I referenced this scripture using the Message Bible translation and not the King James Version. However, just to make sure we are clear in what the Bible is teaching us here, I want you to read it from three more versions (KJV included):

King James Version: "Bless them that curse you, and pray for them which despitefully use you."

Contemporary English Version: "Ask God to bless anyone who curses you, and pray for everyone who is cruel to you."

Amplified Bible: "Invoke blessings upon and pray for the happiness of those who curse you, implore God's blessing (favor) upon those who abuse you [who revile, reproach, disparage, and highhandedly misuse you]"

Could it be any clearer? God wants us to be a blessing to others, period! He wants us to be the love and light in a dark, dying, and decaying world. When people are against you and they give you a hard time, take a few minutes to get away and pray for them.

Pronounce blessings upon them and earnestly pray for God to establish His best upon their lives. If they are giving you a hard time, then they probably need someone to pray for them. Why not be the bigger person and operate in love?

Summary

Praying for those who give you a hard time is a true symbol of Christian maturity. Are you there yet? Can you earnestly pray for those that curse you? Can you sincerely invoke blessings upon those that mistreat you? If you can, then you are operating in the love of God; a love that looks beyond the outward actions of people and sees the need in the person.

*** Notes: Lesson #38 Weekly Reading ***

39. Stay Consistent While under Attack!
Luke 6:28;

"To him who strikes you on the one cheek, offer the other also. And from him, who takes away your cloak, do not withhold your tunic either.

What Jesus is teaching here is that love remains consistent. Love operates in patience. Remember that patience is the ability to endure circumstances while remaining the same. Patience is the "force of consistency."

Matthew explained this. He said, "Here's another old saying that deserves a second look: 'Eye for eye, tooth for tooth.' Is that going to get us anywhere? Here's what I propose: 'Don't hit back at all.' If someone strikes you, stand there and take it" (Matthew 5:38, 39).

The phrase "Eye for an eye, tooth for a tooth" is actually in the Bible. It is in Exodus 21:24; and Leviticus 24:20, but Jesus was contrasting the Old Testament teachings with a New Testament emphasis on the love of God. Jesus was teaching that the love of God enables us to not seek revenge. Webster defines revenge as "the act of inflicting punishment in return for injury or insult." So, this message is not about getting hit in the face and offering to get hit again, it is about not seeking to repay the hit from another with a hit ourselves. Jesus Himself was hit in the face and He did not turn the other cheek, but He also did not hit the person back. We see this in accordance to John 18:22, 23.

As soon as Jesus spoke, one of the temple police hit him and said, "That's no way to talk to the high priest!" Jesus answered, "If I have done something wrong, say so. But if not, why did you hit me?"

Summary

We should not attempt to repay evil with evil. What good is it if we attempt to get revenge for everything people do to us? If we do then how are we different from anyone else? As Christians we are called to be different. We are called to be light in the midst of darkness. We are called to be love in the midst of selfishness.

*** Notes: Lesson #39 Weekly Reading ***

40. Give To Those that Want To Take
Luke 6:29;

> "To him who strikes you on the one cheek, offer the other also. And from him who takes away your cloak, do not withhold your tunic either."

Loving your enemies and praying for those that give you a hard time simply are not natural reactions to mistreatment, but that is exactly the point. When you are born-again, your spirit is renewed with the Holy Spirit, but your mind has yet to be renewed.

In essence, before we can truly operate in biblical faith, our belief system has to change. For example, a man came to Jesus who had a son with a condition that he could address. The man said, "...if you can do anything... help us." Jesus replied, "The issue is not whether or not I can. Everything is possible for him who believes" (Mark 9:22, 23).

In other words, Jesus was saying, "You believe that your son is hopeless because of your current belief system. If you can change your belief system and be open for new possibilities, then I can operate in your life." God wants us to change our belief system that dictates how we deal with people. Instead of repaying evil with evil, we must be reprogrammed to overcome evil with good. Matthew's version helps us understand it better. Matthew said, "... if anyone wants to sue you and take your undershirt (tunic), let him have your coat also" (Matthew 5:40); this was a legal matter.

Jews wore two principal garments, an interior (shirt) and an exterior (coat). The interior garment encircled the whole body and extended down to the knees.

The exterior garment was wrapped around the body and was removed when labor was performed. If an adversary wanted to obtain your interior garment through the legal system, Jesus taught that you should also take your exterior garment, gift wrap it, and give it to him as well rather than follow your normal way of thinking, fighting him tooth-and-nail. Why? Because this is not the way the world operates.

The world goes tit-for-tat against each other and Jesus was teaching us a new way to live. Instead of trying to file a counter lawsuit (or counter argument) for everything, we should seek to operate in God's love to the point where our actions of kindness literally overwhelm the world's actions of treachery.

Summary

You must seek to change the way you look at things. Once you change your perspective and your belief system, you will be open to the leadership of the Holy Spirit concerning how to act and respond to others. Don't respond to evil with evil. Don't respond to malice with more malice. If you do then you are no better than the world. If you are able, however, to renew your mind, then nothing will be impossible to you!

*** Notes: Lesson #40 Weekly Reading ***

41. Give To The Needy
Luke 6:30; AMP

"Give away to everyone who begs of you [who is in want of necessities]..."

I know that the majority of readers are Americans. The United States is a nation of abundance in comparison with most of the world and most Americans do not truly understand how financially blessed they are. I have done a great deal of study on what the Bible has to say about money. The Word has taught me that money makes a great servant, but a poor master. Those that understand the purpose of prosperity are able to keep the proper perspective and use money as a blessing and not a hindrance.

I have heard many teachings on tithing, giving offerings, and supporting ministry. There is another category of biblical giving that is often neglected from our pulpits; and that is giving to the poor. Solomon said, "He who is kind to the poor lends to the Lord, and He will reward him for what he has done." (Proverbs 19:17) He also said, "He who gives to the poor will lack nothing, but he who closes his eyes to them receives many curses." (Proverbs 28:27)

The Bible does say that those who receive a prophet, because they are a prophet, will receive a prophet's reward. This is a direct tie to supporting ministry and ministers and is a text that is often quoted by ministers asking for support.

This is biblical and also something that I perform in my personal life; but I do not neglect the next verse. The next verse says, "And if anyone gives even a cup of cold water to one of these little ones because he is my disciple, I tell you the truth, he will certainly not lose his reward" according to Matthew 10:42.

The point is that you can give without loving, but you cannot love without giving. You cannot love the homeless without wanting to do something for their situation. You cannot truly love the hungry without having the desire to provide them with food. Will you be able to meet every need? Of course not, but love at least wants to help. When you walk in the love of God, you will have a desire to make a difference in the lives of the less fortunate.

Summary

Tithing is good and supporting ministries is fine; but never forget to take the opportunities that the Lord gives you to make a difference in the lives of those less fortunate. There are many organizations that are daily making a difference in people's lives. If you are not postured to impact the needy directly, then at least pray about financially supporting an organization that is.

Remember that what you make happen for others, God will make happen for you!

** Notes: Lesson #41 Weekly Reading ***

42. Practice Benevolence

Luke 6:30; NIV

> "...and if anyone takes what belongs to you, do not demand it back."

Webster defines benevolence as "An inclination to perform kind, charitable acts." We learned in the characteristics of love that love is mindful to do good to others. When you walk in love, you are literally looking for ways to be a blessing to others. One way to be a blessing is to forgive debts.

I know that at first reading it looks as though this text makes reference to those that steal things from you. This is not the case. If someone steals something from you, then they are a thief and you are to treat them as such, but this text makes reference to those that borrow something from you but are having difficulty repaying it. Debt is an epidemic in the United States and is the cause of family problems, high blood pressure, stress, and a myriad of other ailments.

The Israelites knew the dreadful possibilities of debt and the Law established a fail-safe mechanism to ensure that no one would fall into the deadly grips of long-term debt. The Law stated, "At the end of every seventh year, cancel all debts. This is the procedure: Everyone who has lent money to a neighbor writes it off. You must not press your neighbor or his brother for payment: All-Debts-Are-Canceled – GOD says so" According to Deuteronomy 15:1, 2.

Jesus carried this principle of debt cancellation over to the New Testament, but with a twist. You don't have to wait seven years any more. If you lent something to someone and you know that they are struggling to get it back to you, then love simply forgives their debt.

Bless them with it. It will relieve a burden from them and it will give you the satisfaction of walking in the love of God and being a blessing to someone else. Your gift will become a seed and God will cause you to reap a harvest.

Summary

Love does not chase people down to demand that they repay something that they borrowed. If someone has borrowed something from you and it is evident that they are struggling to repay you, consider their situation. If you have no real need of the item, God's love would perhaps lead you to bless them with it. With such an action, you have relieved their burden as well as sown a seed of love.

Love doesn't kick people when they are down; love seeks to pick them up. Be a blessing to someone today. Forgive a debt, share a kind word, make peace with someone you haven't spoken with in a long time, make an effort to do something you know God would want you to do; something you wouldn't normally want to do. As you seek to put God's will above yours, you will find yourself walking in the love of God!

*** Notes: Lesson #42 Weekly Reading ***

43. Practice The Golden Rule
Luke 6:31;

"And just as you want men to do to you, you also do to them likewise."

This action is about sowing and reaping. One of the things highlighted in this series is that Jesus taught this invaluable principle: our harvest is not contingent upon our understanding of the process. In other words, we do not need to totally understand how God will bless us for sowing seeds of love, peace, forgiveness, money, and the rest; but we need to simply believe that we will reap a harvest from our seed.

Jesus said, "God's kingdom is like seed thrown on a field by a man who then goes to bed and forgets about it. The seed sprouts and grows – he has no idea how it happens" According to Mark 4:26, 27. Farmers don't need to a have degree in agriculture to know that if they sow apple seeds they will reap apple trees. They don't need to totally understand the process; they must simply believe the process.

In our text Jesus teaches us a simple rule of thumb. The world calls it the golden rule, but I call it sowing and reaping. If you ask yourself what you want people to do for you and you then take the initiative to do it for them, you are sowing seeds towards your harvest. Paul said, "Don't be misled: No one makes a fool of God. What a person plants, he will harvest."

The person who plants selfishness, ignoring the needs of others ignoring God! – harvests a crop of weeds; All he'll have to show for his life is weeds! But the one who plants in response to God, letting God's Spirit do the growth work in him, harvests a crop of real life, eternal life. So let's not allow ourselves to get fatigued doing good at the right time we will harvest a good crop if we don't give up, or quit" according to Galatians 6:7-9.

Summary

Your harvest is contingent upon your seed, not your full understanding of the process:

You will harvest what you plant. If you do not like your current harvest, you need to check the seed you have been sowing. There is always a space between planting the seed and reaping the harvest. You must remain consistent in that space. You will reap a harvest if you do not give up or quit! Think about how you want others to treat you, then go ahead and treat them that way first – by faith! That's love!

*** Notes: Lesson #43 Weekly Reading ***

44. Love Those Who are Hard to Love
Luke 6:32;

"If you [merely] love those who love you, what quality of credit and thanks is that to you? For even the [very] sinners love their lovers (those who love them)" AMP

The point here is that there should be a clear and distinctive difference between sinners and saints. A hard-core sinner knows how to love those that love them. A person with no relationship with God knows how to return a favor. Those without the Holy Spirit know how to look out for those that look out for them. What makes us different? What makes us distinct? What separates us from the run-of-the-mill sinner? It should be the love of God. Moreover, it should be the love of God in us, on us, and through us; and this love should flow towards all people; not just those that love us back.

There is a difference between agreement and submission. Say, for instance, your wife was hungry and you offered to take her to Taco Bell. To satisfy her hunger, it would require submission on her part, because she does not like fast food. If you offered to take her to Red Lobster to satisfy her hunger then it would not take submission, it would just be a matter of agreement, because she likes Red Lobster. Likewise, when you love those that love you, you are merely agreeing with the person in the action of love.

However, when you love someone who does not love you, you are outwardly displaying your submission and obedience to God. You love them because you are in agreement with God.

Summary

God is not impressed when you love those that love you. He sees that type of love from people who have no relationship with Him. He wants to see you submit yourself to His commandment of love and operate in His love towards those that are hard to love, that cannot stand you, that may even hate you, that treat you wrongly and speak badly of you.

Will you be able to look beyond their feelings for you and obey God's commandment to love? If you can, you are showing your maturity in Christ. God does not reward people who only love those who love them back, but He will reward you when you love those that are hard to love! Are you ready to be blessed? Then walk in the love of God.

*** Notes: Lesson #44 Weekly Reading ***

45. Help Those That Cannot Return the Favor.
Luke 6:33;
"And if you do good to those who do good to you, what credit is that to you? For even sinners do the same."

Scholars tell us that an Israelite is obliged to do good to another Israelite; but they do not have this same obligation towards Gentiles (non-Israelites). An Israelite is not bound to do anything for a Gentile. However, if a Gentile performs an act of goodness or kindness for an Israelite, then the Israelite is bound to show kindness to him and do good to him.

This is a matter of motivation and incentive. Webster defines incentive as, "Something, such as the fear of punishment or the expectation of reward that induces action or motivates effort." The issue here is an expectation of reward. Those that do good for others just because they expect the same in return are seeking an exchange from the person, but Jesus was teaching that our only expectation should be from God.

We ought to want to do good for others just because God is good and He lives in us. His goodness in us should be so strong that it overflows towards others. Not only towards those have been good towards us, but towards those that have never done anything for us and towards those that may never be able to return the favor.

People are anxiously waiting to see a difference in Christians. They want to know if we will act like everyone else or if we will truly live what the Bible says we should live.

Paul said, "All creation is eagerly waiting for God to show who his children are." (Romans 8:19)

We show the world that we are God's children when we act different from the average person and we literally live out what we preach. Our text says that "garden-variety sinners" know how to do good to those that do good to them. Are you any different from a garden-variety sinner? Is God's love in you strong enough to empower you to help those that cannot return the favor?

Summary

Like Abraham, we have been blessed to be a blessing according to Genesis 12:2. This means that God's love has been poured out in our hearts according to Romans 5:5 and it means that we should act like it. Seek to be a blessing to someone today, even if they cannot return the favor. Don't seek your return from them; know that God will bless you for allowing His light to shine through you. Be a blessing with no strings attached!

*** Notes: Lesson #45 Weekly Reading ***

46. Give for Giving's Sake
Luke 6:34

> "And if you lend to those from whom you hope to receive back, what credit is that to you? For even sinners lend to sinners to receive as much back."

Gift giving (in general) is a matter of expectation and pseudo-obligation; one person is expected to bring in a so-called gift and then exchange it with another so-called gift. The problem is that if it requires an exchange, it is not a gift. Webster says that a gift is "something that is bestowed voluntarily and without compensation." By definition then, if it requires compensation, it is not a gift. I see this same pattern played out in my family.

Gifts are given on a regular basis. One family member buys a gift for another family member's baby for his or her birthday. The recipient then feels obligated to get a gift for the other cousin's child's birthday. I've seen this played out for years. I have heard members of my family say, "I wish 'so-and-so' would not have bought this for me.

"Now I have to go and get them something." All of this is done without unction from God. The motivation behind the gifts is more a matter of protocol than sincere benevolence.

If we place an expectation of a return on the person to whom we are giving a gift, then we may be hurting them and not helping them. That's not love. If you are led by love to be a blessing to someone, then you will not expect anything in return. Love gives. You can give without loving, but you cannot love without giving!

Summary

You should give, as God leads you, without any expectation of a return gift. Our text says that if you expect something in return, then you are no different from a pawnbroker. Remember, you can give without loving, but you cannot love without giving!

*** Notes: Lesson #46 Weekly Reading ***

47. Living out Your God –Created Identity
Luke 6:35 AMP

> "But love your enemies and be kind and do good [doing favors] so that someone derives benefit from them] and lend, expecting and hoping for nothing in return but considering nothing as lost and despairing of no one; and then your recompense (your reward) will be great (rich, strong, intense, and abundant), and you will be sons of the Most High, for He is kind and charitable and good to the ungrateful and the selfish and wicked."

Jesus reminds His listeners to love and give knowing that the promised blessing is on the way. This is important because we must understand what happened when we became born-again. At the point of our new birth, our spirit was reborn with God's Spirit, causing us to become children of God. I say children because we, at new birth, are babies in Christ.

In John 1:12 Jesus calls us children of God at this stage. We have a new Spirit, but we do not have a new soul. Our soul is comprised of our mind (thinker), emotions (feeler) and will (chooser). As we grow in Christ and learn to live out our God-created identity, we truly change the way we think about things (mind). We learn how to be led by the Spirit of God and not our feelings (emotions), and we gradually train ourselves to choose (will) things that are pleasing to God. At this stage we graduate from children to actual sonship.

I bring this out because the King James Version of our text promises that if we live this way our "reward shall be great" and that we will be "children of the Highest."

It says children, but it uses a different Greek word than the one used in John 1:12. The Greek word used is "huios." This word is used for those that are mature. This is the same word used in Romans 8:14 where Paul said, "those who are led by the Spirit of God are sons of God". Also used in verse 19 where Paul says, "The creation waits in eager expectation for the sons of God to be revealed."

Summary

Let me attempt to wrap it up in a few nuggets:

When you are born-again you have a new spirit, but your mind, emotions and will (soul) still has to be renewed. At this stage, you are a child (baby) of God. As a new man in an old body you need a new mind. As you walk with God and are led by His Spirit, your thinker, feeler and chooser are transformed and you are then called a son (mature person) of God.

The world is truly waiting for you to act like a son of God. They want to literally "see" people living out what is preached. The world is tired of seeing hypocritical Christians and Paul says they wait in eager expectation for true sons to be revealed.

Walking in love is the greatest litmus test of your spiritual maturity, because God is love. If you think you are mature in Christ, but you cannot walk in love, then you need to reconsider your opinion of yourself. Love is God's greatest expectation!

*** Notes: Lesson #47 Weekly Reading ***

48. Show Mercy
Luke 6:36 AMP

"So be merciful (sympathetic, tender, responsive, and compassionate) even as your Father is [all these]."

Webster says that mercy is "compassionate treatment" and "a disposition to be kind and forgiving." We have already covered in the characteristics of love that love is mindful to do good towards others. Let's take love to the next level by our action, showing mercy which takes us further towards forgiveness.

I often say that we ought to continually give God praise for His grace and mercy. Grace is God giving us what we do not deserve. Mercy is God not giving us what we do deserve. Lamentations tells us that "The Lord's kindness never fails! If he had not been merciful, we would have been destroyed. The Lord can always be trusted to show mercy each morning" according to Lamentations 3:22, 23. Think about that for a moment. God is faithful to show us mercy. If the Lord had truly given us everything we deserved, for every action (good and bad); then we might not be here today. I thank God that He showed mercy on me when I messed up and I thank God that the Bible says I can trust Him to show me mercy every morning!

The King James Version of this text tells me that His mercies are literally renewed every morning. I don't have to face today with yesterday's mercy. That is awesome. That gives us hope. That helps us understand how much God cares about us and how He is faithful to forgive us.

If God will do all this for us, then should we not show the same mercy and forgiveness towards others? Jesus told a story in Matthew 18:21-35 about a servant who failed to understand this principle. This guy owed a large sum of money, in the hundreds of thousands of dollars, and he could not pay it back. He was about to lose his family when his master had a change of heart and decided to forgive all his debt. This was awesome!

The guy then left that place and ran into another person who owed him a few dollars and he wound up choking the man, demanding payment, and having him imprisoned. When the servant's master found out about it he was furious. The master came back to the servant and had him tortured until he could pay the entire original debt back. Jesus then said, "This is how my Heavenly Father will treat each of you unless you forgive your brother from your heart" (verse 35).

Summary

The message is simple: forgive just like God forgave you. Show mercy towards others, just like God shows mercy towards you. When you act like God, you are walking in His love!

*** Notes: Lesson #48 Weekly Reading ***

49. Don't Pick On Others
Luke 6:37

> "Judge not, and ye shall not be judged: condemn not, and ye shall not be condemned: forgive, and ye shall be forgiven."

The Bible has a great deal to say about love.

1. **Don't pick on people:** To pick on someone is to intentionally cause undue stress; to hassle, annoy and irritate. Have you ever met someone who constantly harasses others? I don't mean the person who jokingly plays around, but the one that finds pleasure in intentionally aggravating other people? These people are constantly seeking to identify contentious areas in the lives of others and when they find them, they take every opportunity to "push their buttons." The bottom line is that love does not act that way. Love seeks to minimize and not magnify the weaknesses of others.

2. **Don't focus on their failures:** Failure is a part of life. I am a person who is not accustomed to failure, but we all have to deal with it. Most millionaires have filed for bankruptcy at least once.

What does that mean? It means that they have failed, but they recovered from their failure. Dr. John Maxwell wrote a book entitled "Failing Forward". It certainly blessed me when I was down.

I recovered and so can others, but it is more difficult to recover when there are others waiting to focus on your failure and constantly re mind you of your mistakes. These people do not help and we should not be one of them.

3. **Don't criticize their faults:** You may be in the position where you lead others. Part of your responsibility may be to "identify" the faults of your subordinates. There is a difference between identifying and criticizing a fault. This goes beyond a normal critique and gets into the harassment arena. Don't be one of these people.

4. **Unless you want the same treatment:** Always remember the principle of sowing and reaping. In the world they say, "What goes around comes around." This is truly a biblical principle and you will reap what you sow (**Galatians 6:7**). Whatever you bring into being for others good or bad – you are, in reality, creating the same for yourself.

Summary

We all endure hardships from time to time and there are times in our lives where we feel like we have been picked out to be picked on. People have enough to deal with in the course of their lives already; they do not need anyone else putting any external pressures on them. As a Christian, you should be there to help and not to hurt, to be a blessing and not a burden.

*** Notes: Lesson #49 Weekly Reading ***

50. Don't Condemn the Downtrodden
Luke 6:37

> "Judge not, and you shall not be judged. Condemn not, and you shall not be condemned. Forgive, and you will be forgiven."

Jesus clearly explained this issue of judgment in Matthew, chapter 7 when He said, "Do not judge, or you too will be judged. For in the same way you judge others, you will be judged, and with the measure you use, it will be measured to you.

Why do you look at the speck of sawdust in your brother's eye and pay no attention to the plank in your own eye? How can you say to your brother, 'Let me take the speck out of your eye,' when all the time there is a plank in your own eye? You hypocrite, first take the plank out of your own eye, and then you will see clearly to remove the speck from your brother's eye." (Verses 1-5 NIV)

The point here is that love focuses on others for the purpose of being a blessing, but it focuses on self when it comes time for judgment. Love ensures that we keep a proper perspective of ourselves. Those that are babes in Christ are often the ones that are quick to judge. Seasoned believers seem to be less judgmental. Why? Because the more you know about Christ, the less you think of yourself. The more you know about the many times that God covered you with His grace and mercy, the less critical you will be of the mistakes of others.

Summary

Love is there to pick up those who are down, not to kick them down further. Paul said, "Those of us who are strong and able in the faith need to step in and lend a hand to those who falter, and not just do what is most convenient for us. Strength is for service, not status." (Romans 15:1).

Are you in Christ for service? If so, then you will be there to help and not to hurt those who are down. Pick someone up today. Pick them up with a smile, kind word, a listening ear or a few moments to show that you care. People don't care how much you know until they know how much you care! Show God's love today.

*** Notes: Lesson #50 Weekly Reading ***

51. Be Easy on People
Luke 6:37

"Judge not, and you shall not be judged. Condemn not, and you shall not be condemned. Forgive, and you will be forgiven."

You never know, a person may be hard, rude and resentful and needs to hear a kind word or they may be a pleasant, soft, and considerate person who is simply having a bad day. In either case, if we go easy on them, we can help change their day and maybe even their life for the better. Self-centered people cannot do great things for God. They miss the opportunities that God presents to them, because they are constantly focused on their problems, issues and concerns. If your perspective is always on you, then you will never see what God needs you to see in your spouse, child, or coworker.

When someone gives you a hard time, instead of striking back, think about them for a moment. What might they be going through? Are they stressed? Are they overwhelmed? Are they dealing with personal pressure? You never know what they are facing. Other versions of this text say, "Forgive, and you will be forgiven." The quicker you forgive them, the quicker you will be able to look beyond their actions and ask them:

How are you? Is everything alright? You can surprise them by replying to their harsh treatment by saying something nice such as: "I like that shirt, where did you get it?" or, "You sure look nice today." You will soon find this verse will come alive in your life. As you are easy on people, your life will be a great deal better.

Summary

Walking in the love of God is more than just lip service. We all have bad days. I have had my fair share of challenges in life and I haven't always been as nice as I should have been. I was convicted about it, repented and then moved forward. In times past, perhaps if I had been easier on people, I would have gotten the issue resolved quicker.

The good thing is I learned a phrase a few years ago that changed my life forever, "Yesterday ended last night!" No matter how you treated people yesterday, it's over. This is a new day with new mercy according to Lamentations 3:23. Determine to do better. Be easy on people and your life will be easier for you.

*** Notes: Lesson #51 Weekly Reading ***

52. Live to Give and You Want Regret It
Luke 6:38

> "Give, and it shall be given unto you; good measure, pressed down, and shaken together, and running over, shall men give into your bosom. For with the same measure that ye mete withal it shall be measured to you again."

This text is used in pulpits all over the world on a regular basis when the offering is being received. A more common translation (NIV) of the text says, "Give, and it will be given to you."

We commonly use this to refer to money and it does apply to money; "Give away your life…" After dealing with things like loving your enemies, doing good to those that mistreat you and praying for those that give you a hard time, Jesus returns to this issue of sowing and reaping. He promises that your actions will not go unrewarded. More than likely, your natural inclination will not be to love your enemies or pray for those that give you a hard time; but if you put these 17 actions of love into practice then you will literally be changing your composition. You will force yourself into becoming "transformed" into the image and likeness of Christ according to Romans 12:1, 2, by renewing your mind to think like He thinks and act like He acts. If you do this, our text says that you will literally be giving your life away. What it truly means is that you will be giving your old and evil tendencies away and replacing them with the characteristics of the God of love, peace and joy. Will you still be you? Of course! But a new you, with a new attitude, a new perspective, and a new life!

Summary

You should live to give. Give your life to Christ. Give your love to others. Give forgiveness to those that hurt you, mercy to those that mistreat you and help to those that need it. As you live to give you will find that you will not regret it.

God will give you peace in your heart, clarity in your mind, strength in your body, vision for your family, provision for the vision and an overflowing return on every good seed sown! Walk in love and your life will be changed for the better!

*** Notes: Lesson #52 Weekly Reading ***

List of all Scriptures used in this book

1 Corinthians 10:12, 13
1 Corinthians 12:31
1 Corinthians 13:4;
1 Corinthians 13:6 AMP
1 John 1:9
1 John 3:23
1 John 5:3
1 Peter 5:5
1 Samuel 16:7
1 Timothy 1:5 AMP
Daniel 10:21
Deuteronomy 32:4
Ephesians 4:32
Exodus 3:14
Ezekiel 36:25-27
Galatians 6:7
Genesis 12:2
John 1:12
John 11:35
John 13:34, 35
John 16:13
John 8:44
Joshua 1:8
Leviticus 24:20
Luke 23:34
Luke 6:29
Luke 6:32
Luke 6:34
Luke 6:38
Mark 9:22, 23
Matthew 12:34
Matthew 18:7
Matthew 5:38, 39
Proverbs 16:18
Proverbs 19:17
Proverbs 28:27
Psalm 139:13, 14
Psalm 19:14

1 Corinthians 12:26
1 Corinthians 13:1-3;
1 Corinthians 13:4-8;
1 Corinthians 13:7 AMP
1 John 2:16
1 John 4:8
1 Peter 4:8 AMP
1 Peter 5:7
1 Thessalonians 5:23
2 Corinthians 5:21
Deuteronomy 15:1, 2
Ephesians 2:2, 3
Exodus 21:24
Ezekiel 11:19 AMP
Galatians 5:22
Galatians 6:7-9
Isaiah 14:13, 14
John 1:14
John 13:34
John 14:17
John 21:15-17
Lamentations 3:22, 23
Lamentations 3:23
Luke 15:22, 23
Luke 6:27
Luke 6:30; NIV
Luke 6:33;
Luke 6:37
Mark 4:26, 27
Matthew 10:42
Matthew 18:21-35
Matthew 22:37-39
Proverbs 10:12
Proverbs 19:17
Proverbs 23:7
Psalm 1:3
Psalm 19:1
Psalm 19:4

Romans 10:9, 10
Romans 12:15 AMP
Romans 15:1
Romans 5:5-8
Romans 7:14-25
Romans 8:19
Romans 8:35-39

Romans 12:1, 2
Romans 12:4, 5
Romans 5:5
Romans 5:8
Romans 7:15
Romans 8:29

Are you ready to experience the Love of God? In obedience to Jesus, Matthew 11:28-30 says…"Come and Learn of Me" If your answer is yes, on the next few Pages there is a list of scriptures to help you to <u>establish</u> a relationship with the God and become a citizen of the Kingdom through receiving His only begotten Son Jesus who is the Christ.

Decision of Love

God's Word has the power to literally transform your life, recreate the heart of a person, change how they and secure their eternity.

To receive Jesus Christ as your own personal Lord and Savior

Are you born again? Have you ever received Jesus as your Lord and Savior? If the answer to this question is no, read these scriptures and pray this prayer, agreeing with it and believing it from your heart

John 3:16 "For God so loved the world, that he gave his only begotten Son, that whosoever believeth in him should not perish, but have everlasting life"

Romans 10:9-10, 13 "That if thou shalt confess with thy mouth the Lord Jesus, and shalt believe in thine heart that God hath raised him from the dead, thou shalt be saved. For whosoever shall call upon the name of the Lord shall be saved.

For with the heart man believeth unto righteousness; and with the mouth **Confession** is made unto salvation.

John 14:6 " Jesus said unto him, I am the way, the truth and the life: no man cometh unto the Father, but by me."

Pray this pray now to Receive Salvation

Dear God,

I want to become a citizen of your Kingdom. I come to you in the name of Jesus, your son. I confess I am a sinner. I believe you sent your son to die on the cross for my sins. I confess with my mouth that Jesus Christ is Lord. Thank you for allowing me to become a Christian; I am translated from the kingdom of darkness to the Kingdom of God.

In Jesus' name I pray, Amen!

A genuine born-again Christian, a citizen of the Kingdom of God wants, above everything else, to do the will of God. Don't be ashamed to witness to others and tell them how to become a Christian. Join a Bible believing Church and be water baptized as an act of faith to let the world know you are following Christ's example.

Signed _____

Date _____

If you would like to receive the Holy Spirit, ask the Father in Jesus' name to fill you with the Holy Spirit. Believe you receive when you ask, and begin to speak your new language in faith as God gives it to you.

Pray this pray now to Receive the fullness of the Holy Spirit

Heavenly Father,

I come to you in faith, believing that Jesus Christ died in my place, for my sins, and arose from the dead. I ask you to fill me to overflowing with the Holy Spirit. You said in your Word that if I asked I would receive, so I ask you now to fill me to overflowing with your precious Holy Spirit. I receive Him now by faith and expect to speak with other tongues as he gives me the utterance. In Jesus' Name Amen

Pray this pray now to Receive your healing

Now I want you to pray for your healing. Put your hand on your body where you are sick and repeat this prayer: Lord Jesus you are the Great Physician. All healing comes from you. By your stripes we are healed. I speak your Word over this body and thank you that you heal all our diseases. Thank you for healing and enabling me to walk in health. In Jesus' Name Amen

About the Author

Pastor James L. Monteria is born again, an ordained Pastor and Teacher of the Gospel of Lord Jesus Christ. Pastor James L. Monteria is a graduate of Rhema Bible Training Center of Broken Arrow a suburb of Tulsa, Oklahoma.

Pastor Monteria received his Bachelor of Science Degree in Business Administration from Saint Paul's College in Lawrenceville, VA. He received a Master's Degree in Instructional Education from Central Michigan University, Mount Pleasant, Michigan.

Pastor Monteria has ministered the Word of God through seminars, church services, Bible studies, Prison Ministries, distribution of his books and tapes. Pastor Monteria believes that the Bible is the Word of God, and he is an anointed Pastor and Teacher of the Word of God.

His ministries are combination of anointed Preaching and Teaching the Word of God, and flowing in the gifts of the Holy Spirit as the lead.

Pastor J. L. Monteria is available

~Speaking Engagements~
~Book Signings~
~Workshops\Conferences~

You may contact J L Monteria via
Email: Clmpublication.info@gmail.com

Postal Mail:
P.O. Box 932 Chesterfield, VA 23832
Website: www.clmpublication.info

www.ingramcontent.com/pod-product-compliance
Lightning Source LLC
Chambersburg PA
CBHW061759110426
42742CB00012BB/2192